To Dear
Jennifer
Love from
Grandma & Grandpa.
Feb 19/92

the *Vegetarian* cookbook

the *Vegetarian* cookbook

Carol Bowen

CHANCELLOR
PRESS

Acknowledgments

The author and publisher would like to thank the following companies
for their help in supplying some of the recipes and photographs for this book:

Apple and Pear Development Council (pages 63, 148, 149)

Anchor Foods

Batchelors Foods (pages 67, 131)

Billingtons Sugars

California Raisin Advisory Board (pages 47, 59, 116, 123)

Colman's of Norwich (pages 51, 152, 155, 177)

Danish Dairy Board (pages 50, 68, 69, 123, 151, 168)

Flour Advisory Bureau

Food and Wine from France (pages 76, 80)

Gale's Honey and Curds (pages 145, 146, 153, 154, 155, 156, 169, 187)

Green Giant Company

H. J. Heinz Company Ltd (pages 75, 130)

Jif Lemon Bureau (pages 155, 157)

Kellogg's (page 109)

MCP Food Group for Broadland Vegetable Suet (page 183)

Milk Marketing Board (pages 62, 64, 93, 101, 129, 130)

Mushroom Growers' Association (page 95)

Pasta Information Centre (page 61)

Summer Orange Office (Outspan) (page 99)

U.S.A. Pecans (pages 57, 172)

U.S. Rice Council (pages 56, 57, 81)

Weight Watchers from Heinz (pages 137, 139, 140, 141)

Jacket photography: Octopus Publishing Group, Roger Stowell
All remaining photography: Chris Crofton
Home economist: Lyn Rutherford
Stylist: Andrea Lambton

This edition published in 1991 by
Chancellor Press
Michelin House
81 Fulham Road
London SW3 6RB

ISBN 1 85152 116 X

Produced by Mandarin Offset
Printed in Hong Kong

A catalogue record for this book is available
from the British Library

Contents

Useful facts and figures

Notes on metrication

In this book quantities are given in metric and Imperial measures. Exact conversion from Imperial to metric measures does not usually give very convenient working quantities and so the metric measures have been rounded off into units of 25 grammes. The table below shows the recommended equivalents.

Ounces	Approx g to nearest whole figure	Recommended conversion to nearest unit of 25
1	28	25
2	57	50
3	85	75
4	113	100
5	142	150
6	170	175
7	198	200
8	227	225
9	255	250
10	283	275
11	312	300
12	340	350
13	368	375
14	396	400
15	425	425
16 (1 lb)	454	450
17	482	475
18	510	500
19	539	550
20 (1¼ lb)	567	575

Note: When converting quantities over 20 oz first add the appropriate figures in the centre column, then adjust to the nearest unit of 25. As a general guide, 1 kg (1000 g) equals 2.2 lb or about 2 lb 3 oz. This method of conversion gives good results in nearly all cases, although in certain pastry and cake recipes a more accurate conversion is necessary to produce a balanced recipe.

Liquid measures The millilitre has been used in this book and the following table gives a few examples.

Imperial	Approx ml to nearest whole figure	Recommended ml
¼ pint	142	150 ml
½ pint	283	300 ml
¾ pint	425	450 ml
1 pint	567	600 ml
1½ pints	851	900 ml
1¾ pints	992	1000 ml (1 litre)

Spoon measures All spoon measures given in this book are level unless otherwise stated.

Can sizes At present, cans are marked with the exact (usually to the nearest whole number) metric equivalent of the Imperial weight of the contents, so we have followed this practice when giving can sizes.

Egg sizes All eggs used refer to sizes 3 or 4 unless otherwise stated. Sizes 1 and 2 refer to large eggs and sizes 4 to 6 refer to small eggs.

Flour All flour used is plain (U.S. all-purpose flour) unless otherwise stated.

NOTE: **When making any of the recipes in this book, follow only one set of measures as they are not interchangeable.**

Honey muffins (recipe page 162)

Notes for American and Australian users

In America the 8-oz measuring cup is used. In Australia metric measures are now used in conjunction with the standard 250-ml measuring cup. The Imperial pint, used in Britain and Australia, is 20 fl oz, while the American pint is 16 fl oz. It is important to remember that the Australian tablespoon differs from both the British and American tablespoons; the table below gives a comparison. The British standard tablespoon, which has been used throughout this book, holds 17.7 ml, the American 14.2 ml, and the Australian 20 ml. A teaspoon holds approximately 5 ml in all three countries.

British	American	Australian
1 teaspoon	1 teaspoon	1 teaspoon
1 tablespoon	1 tablespoon	1 tablespoon
2 tablespoons	2–3 tablespoons	2 tablespoons
3½ tablespoons	4 tablespoons	3 tablespoons
4 tablespoons	5 tablespoons	3½ tablespoons

An Imperial/American guide to solid and liquid measures

Imperial	American	Imperial	American
Solid measures		**Liquid measures**	
1 lb butter or margarine	2 cups	¼ pint liquid	⅔ cup liquid
1 lb flour	4 cups	½ pint	1¼ cups
1 lb granulated or castor sugar	2 cups	¾ pint	2 cups
1 lb icing sugar	3 cups	1 pint	2½ cups
8 oz rice	1 cup	1½ pints	3¾ cups
		2 pints	5 cups (2½ pints)

American terms

The list below gives some American equivalents or substitutes for terms and ingredients used in this book:

British/American
Equipment and terms
pastry case/pie shell
baking tin/roasting tin
baking tray/baking or cookie sheet
cling film/Saran wrap
deep cake tin/springform pan
flan/open or single crusted pie
flan tin or ring/pie pan
frying pan/skillet
greaseproof paper/waxed paper
grill/broil
minced/ground
palette knife/spatula
patty tins/muffin pans
pudding basin/ovenproof bowl or pudding mold
sandwich tin/layer cake pan
stoned/pitted
Swiss roll tin/jelly roll pan

British/American
Ingredients
apple purée/applesauce
aubergine/eggplant
beetroot/beets
bicarbonate or soda/baking soda
biscuits/crackers or cookies
black olives/ripe olives
broad beans/fava or lima beans
chocolate, plain/chocolate, semi-sweet
desiccated coconut/shredded coconut
cornflour/cornstarch
courgettes/zucchini
cream, single/cream, light
cream, double/cream, heavy
digestive biscuits/graham crackers
flour, plain/flour, all-purpose
flour, self-raising/flour sifted with baking powder
fresh yeast/compressed yeast
hard-boiled eggs/hard-cooked eggs
haricot beans/navy beans
marrow/summer squash
mandarins and satsumas/tangerines
shortcrust pastry/basic pie dough
soured cream/dairy sour cream
sponge finger biscuits/ladyfingers
spring onion/scallion
icing sugar/confectioner's sugar
castor sugar/superfine sugar
sultanas/golden raisins
swede/rutabaga
tomato purée/tomato paste
yeast, dried/active dry yeast
yogurt, natural/yogurt, plain

Foreword

Confessions first – I am not a committed vegetarian of many years' standing. No, I'm more what I call a would-be vegetarian – one of an ever-increasing group of people who, for a wide variety of reasons, find they prefer to eat less meat, fish and poultry and eat more vegetables and fruit.

Over the years I have learnt a great deal about vegetarian foods. I now eat much less meat and prefer my diet this way. The transition to vegetarianism can be a slow process, but providing your diet is well-balanced it need not be a shock to your system. You will find that your meals are exciting, delicious and extremely versatile.

So I hope this book will inspire you to create dishes to appeal to everyone whether cooking for the family or friends.

CAROL BOWEN

Introduction

Eating for health

Vegetarian cooking isn't cranky cooking as millions of new followers will testify – it's simply nutritious healthy cooking without meat, fish or poultry. And it's gaining popularity – so much so that the number of vegetarians has increased ten-fold in the last 10 years.

Mainly for health, social or economic reasons people are turning to vegetarian 'meatless' meals as a total replacement for, or as a partial alternative to, the traditional meat-and-two-vegetable family meal. So much so that vegetarian eating is viewed with respect especially since it also reflects and puts into practise many of the recommendations that nutritionists advise for healthy living. In fact when a vegetarian diet is properly balanced it has many virtues and few set-backs.

Balance of course is the keyword – for anyone who chooses to abstain from one or more types of food in addition denies him or herself the nutrients it provides. It is reasonably simple to provide a good well-balanced diet for the majority of vegetarians – or at least those who simply do not eat meat, fish and poultry, yet still eat eggs and dairy produce. Not quite so straightforward for vegans who do not eat eggs, honey or dairy products in addition to meat, poultry and fish.

For balance the following nutrients must be supplied to the body:

Proteins play a vital role in body maintenance, growth and repair. They also can be used to provide energy.

Fats The real high-energy providers but also insulators of body heat.

Carbohydrates Energy providers too but cellulose, and a carbohydrate, giving bulk and fibre to the diet.

Vitamins are required for body building and maintenance, to assist in the metabolism of other nutrients and in general to provide resistance to infection and disease.

Minerals are necessary for the proper growth, development and maintenance of the body and its organs and the functioning of muscles.

In essence, and at its simplest, fats and carbohydrates are the body's principle sources of energy. Proteins can also provide energy but along with vitamins and minerals their prime function is in body building and maintenance.

To achieve an adequate diet there must be balance between the three major nutrients – proteins, fats and carbohydrates. Proteins are of prime importance; it is judged that a person should eat $85\,\text{g}/3\frac{1}{2}$ oz protein a day,

about 10 per cent of the total energy intake. More than that would simply be converted into fat for energy. Sounds simple until we consider that not all proteins are alike and some are nutritionally superior to others – the ones that supply the essential amino acids. A balance of amino acids is also needed in the daily diet. A diet should therefore be varied enough to ensure an adequate and comprehensive supply across the range of amino acids required.

That leaves fats and carbohydrates to consider. Both are energy providers and fats also supply many fat-soluble vitamins as part of their makeup. The consensus of opinion today recommends that we do not exceed the respectable level of $80\,\text{g}/3$ oz fat per day, that is about 30 per cent of our energy intake. Carbohydrates can take care of the rest – but again here there are recommendations. Carbohydrates should be increasingly of the less refined or high-fibre type rather than the super-rich refined sugars or carbohydrates that are super-low on nutrients.

Finally a balance must be achieved in supplying adequate vitamins and minerals for good health. However, in the main, if we balance our diet by eating a good versatile range of fats, carbohydrates and proteins there will be an adequate supply of vitamins and minerals.

Vegetarians will find protein in eggs, vegetables, cheese, milk, grains, pulses, nuts and seeds; fats in cheese, milk and other dairy produce, nuts, vegetable oils, spreads and eggs; carbohydrates in sugars and syrups, fruit and vegetables, cereals, pulses and grains; and vitamins and minerals in almost every food but they are especially rich in fruit and vegetables.

Introducing such foods to replace traditional meat, fish and poultry to the diet is not initially easy and should be done gradually. Start by substituting say eggs, cheese, beans, lentils, vegetables and nuts for meat, poultry and fish. Instead of using lard opt for butter, a vegetable oil spread or margarine. Try eating whole grains, cereals, wholewheat pasta and pulses instead of refined white flour, polished rice, white bread and refined breakfast cereals. And in essence lean heavily towards fresh fruit and vegetables as your anchor for an infinite source of meal and nutrient variety.

There is a different fruit or vegetable that comes into its peak supply for every month of the year. Follow the seasons as your best and most reliable guide to finding tasty, economical and flavoursome foods month after month – nature will ensure they also provide the virtues of variety.

Guide to the best of foods in season

January
Fruit Grapefruit, Seville oranges, tangerines, lemons, limes, rhubarb, cranberries
Vegetables Brussels sprouts, onions, carrots, celery, leeks, parsnips, red cabbage, turnips, broccoli

February
Fruit Grapefruit, lemons, limes, oranges, tangerines, rhubarb, Seville oranges
Vegetables Broccoli, Brussels sprouts, cabbage, cauliflower, celery, leeks, parsnips, red cabbage, turnips

March
Fruit Grapefruit, lemons, oranges, rhubarb
Vegetables Broccoli, Brussels sprouts, cauliflower, cabbage, celery, chicory (U.S. endive), Jerusalem artichokes, leeks, parsnips, turnips, swedes (U.S. rutabagas), watercress

April
Fruit Grapefruit, lemons, oranges, pineapple, rhubarb
Vegetables Purple sprouting, broccoli, chicory (U.S. endive), leeks, parsnips, spinach, garlic, watercress, lettuce, spring onions (U.S. scallions)

May
Fruit Apricots, gooseberries, lemons, oranges, pineapple, rhubarb
Vegetables Asparagus, broad beans (U.S. fava or lima beans), broccoli, carrots, cauliflower, courgettes (U.S. zucchini), globe artichokes, peas, spinach, herbs, watercress, fennel, spring onions (U.S. scallions), lettuce, radishes

June
Fruit Apricots, gooseberries, lemons, loganberries, oranges, peaches, raspberries, rhubarb, strawberries, cherries, avocado pears
Vegetables Asparagus, broad beans (U.S. fava or lima beans), cabbage, cauliflower, corn-on-the-cob, courgettes (U.S. zucchini), French beans, globe artichokes, peas, potatoes, spinach, tomatoes, lettuce, spring onions (U.S. scallions), radishes

July
Fruit Apricots, blackcurrants, cherries, figs, gooseberries, lemons, loganberries, melons, nectarines, oranges, peaches, plums, raspberries, redcurrants, strawberries, avocado pears
Vegetables Aubergines (U.S. eggplants), broad beans (U.S. fava or lima beans), calabrese, cabbage, carrots, cauliflower, corn-on-the-cob, courgettes (U.S. zucchini), French beans, globe artichokes, peas, peppers, potatoes, spinach, tomatoes, lettuce, radishes, spring onions (U.S. scallions), watercress, cucumbers

August
Fruit Apples, blackberries, damsons, greengages, melons, plums, peaches, strawberries, raspberries, pears
Vegetables Aubergines (U.S. eggplants), cabbage, cauliflower, corn-on-the-cob, courgettes (U.S. zucchini), French beans, globe artichokes, marrow (U.S. summer squash), peas, peppers, runner beans (U.S. green beans), spinach, tomatoes, cress

September
Fruit Apples, blackberries, damsons, grapes, lemons, oranges, peaches, pears, plums, melons
Vegetables Aubergines (U.S. eggplants), cabbage, cauliflower, celery, corn-on-the-cob, courgettes (U.S. zucchini), leeks, marrow (U.S. summer squash), onions, parsnips, peppers, runner beans (U.S. green beans), spinach, swedes (U.S. rutabagas), tomatoes

October
Fruit Apples, blackberries, damsons, grapes, lemons, figs, oranges, pears, pomegranates, pumpkin, quinces, dates, nuts
Vegetables Broccoli, Brussels sprouts, cabbage, celery, leeks, marrow (U.S. summer squash), parsnips, red cabbage, spinach, swedes (U.S. rutabagas), turnips, corn-on-the-cob, onions

November
Fruit Apples, cranberries, grapes, lemons, oranges, pears, tangerines, clementines, satsumas, pomegranates, kiwi fruit (U.S. Chinese gooseberries), dates, nuts
Vegetables Brussels sprouts, cabbage, carrots, celery, chicory (U.S. endive), Jerusalem artichokes, parsnips, red cabbage, spinach, swedes (U.S. rutabagas), turnips, mushrooms, onions, potatoes

December
Fruit Apples, cranberries, grapes, lemons, bananas, oranges, pears, pomegranates, tangerines, nuts
Vegetables Brussels sprouts, cabbage, carrots, celery, chicory (U.S. endive), Jerusalem artichokes, leeks, parsnips, red cabbage, spinach, swedes (U.S. rutabagas), turnips

Mixed bean casserole (recipe page 130)

Wheat, whole grain

Cracked wheat

Wheat flakes

Wholewheat flour

Wheatmeal flour

Unbleached white flour

Barley, whole grain

Barley flakes

Barley flour

Popcorn

Cornmeal

Oats, whole grain

Rolled oat flakes

Oatmeal

White rice

Basmati rice

Wild rice

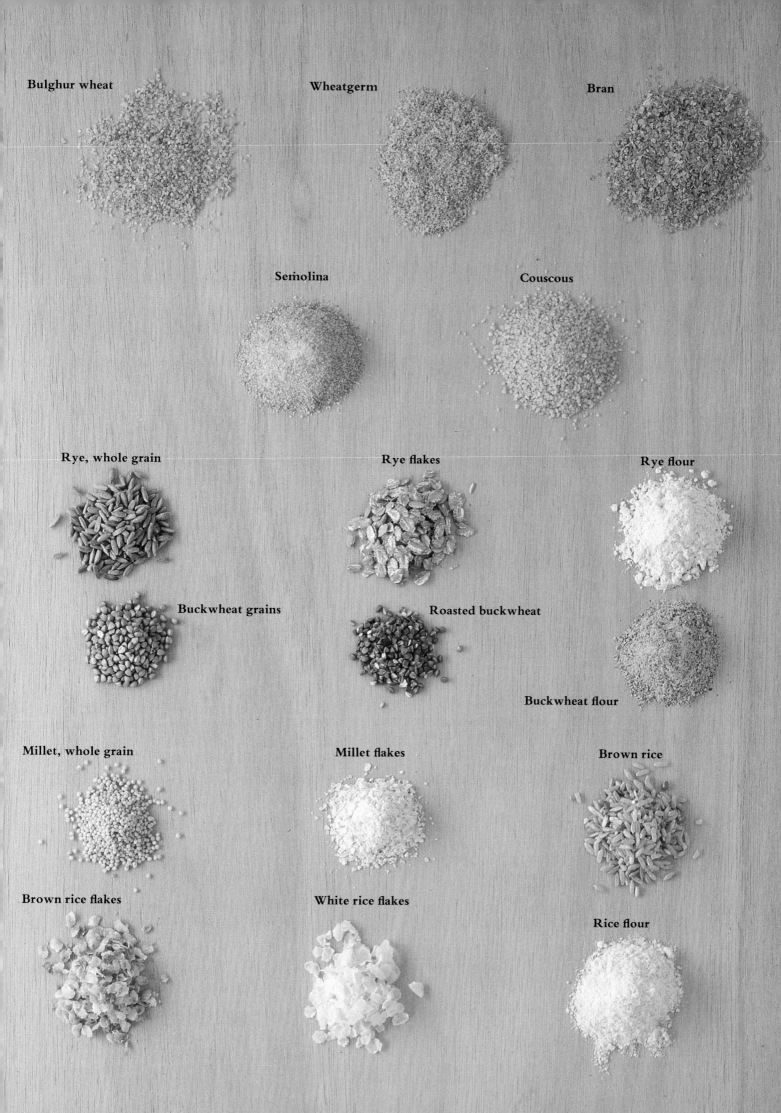

Bulghur wheat

Wheatgerm

Bran

Semolina

Couscous

Rye, whole grain

Rye flakes

Rye flour

Buckwheat grains

Roasted buckwheat

Buckwheat flour

Millet, whole grain

Millet flakes

Brown rice

Brown rice flakes

White rice flakes

Rice flour

A–Z of vegetarian foods

Grains

Barley A grain that is principally used in brewing and the making of baby foods. In Europe the grain is mainly eaten as pearl barley or pot barley. Pot barley is the whole grain minus the outer husk.

Barley flakes Produced by rolling the whole grain into flat flakes for quicker cooking.

Barley flour A fine sweet flour that adds a distinctive taste to breads and biscuits (u.s. cookies).

Bran The tough outer coating of the whole wheat grain which is removed during processing. It is valuable for its fibre but also contains B vitamins and phosphorus.

Buckwheat The whole grain also called saracen corn.

Buckwheat flour A heavy, strong and savoury flour made from buckwheat. Many recipes call for it to be mixed with other flours such as rice or wheat to lighten it.

Buckwheat, roasted The crushed and hulled seeds of the plant buckwheat that have been roasted to give a nutty flavour.

Cornmeal Also called maize meal and polenta, available as fine and coarse meal.

Couscous A cereal processed from semolina. Used principally in the North African dish bearing the same name.

Flour, wheatmeal A flour where most but not all of the wheatgerm and bran have been removed.

Flour, white, unbleached A flour where all of the wheatgerm and bran have been removed. The flour has not however been chemically treated.

Flour, wholewheat A flour made from the whole grain, available stoneground or roller-milled.

Millet Probably the first cereal grain to be used for domestic purposes. Available in many varieties from foxtail to prosso.

Millet flakes Produced by rolling the whole grain. Use in cereals or where rice flakes may be used.

Oats The whole grain, rarely used as such for cooking because of its long cooking time.

Oat flakes, rolled Produced by rolling the softened whole oat grain.

Oatmeal Produced by rolling and grinding the softened whole oat grain. Often available in three grades, fine, coarse and medium. It is generally used for making porridge or muesli (u.s. granola) but can be added to bread, cakes and biscuits (u.s. cookies).

Popcorn Corn or maize grains. A variety with an especially hard endosperm is called popcorn.

Rice, basmati A narrow long-grain white rice with a fine flavour. A favourite in Indian cuisine.

Rice, brown A whole long or short grain rice where only the indigestible husks have been removed.

Rice flakes, brown Brown rice flaked by processing for quick cooking.

Rice flakes, white White rice powder flaked to make a quick-cooking product.

Rice flour Usually made from white flour, including some bran. Popular for use as a thickening agent and for making cakes and biscuits (u.s. cookies).

Rice, white A polished long or short grain rice where the husk, germ and outer layers have been removed in processing.

Rice, wild Not really a rice at all but looking very much like one. It is an expensive grain, that needs a long cooking time, but superior nutty flavour.

Rye The whole grain or groats. Used in bread-making especially in Eastern Europe.

Rye flakes Produced by rolling the whole grain. Used in making muesli (u.s. granola) and other breakfast cereals.

Rye flour Available dark or light (shown on page 13). Dark rye flour is made from the whole grain, light rye flour uses partially husked rye grains.

Semolina A product of the starchy part of the wheat grain. Available as medium or coarse meal.

Wheat The whole grain or berry (shown on page 12). There are many kinds but they can be generally divided into soft and hard varieties. Hard is used for bread and pasta making, soft for cake and biscuit (u.s. cookie) making.

Wheat, bulghur A cooked, par-boiled wheat that needs little extra cooking.

Wheat, cracked Produced by cracking the whole grain by pressure machines. This process ensures the grain cooks faster.

Wheat flakes Produced by rolling the whole grain to a flat shape. This process also ensures speedier cooking.

Wheatgerm A valuable constituent of the whole grain wheat that is removed during some processing, it is particularly rich in the B complex vitamins and vitamin E. It is usually available in three forms: as natural wheatgerm; stabilized wheatgerm; or wheatgerm oil.

Nuts and seeds

Almonds, blanched where the skin has been removed to reveal the white flesh.

Almonds in shell Only the sweet variety can be eaten since bitter almonds contain poisonous prussic acid.

Almonds, shelled to reveal the kernel. Use in making cakes, biscuits (U.S. cookies), desserts and savoury dishes.

Almonds, slivered or sliced for adding to salads, cakes, biscuits (U.S. cookies) and savoury main dishes.

Brazil nuts in shell Also known as the para or cream nut, the Brazil nut has a tough, angular shell.

Brazil nuts, shelled to reveal the brown-skinned creamy-white kernel.

Cashew nuts, shelled Generally found only this way since the shell contains an acrid fluid which blisters the skin.

Chestnuts in shell The large brown nut of the Castenea tree. There are over 100 sweet varieties to choose from.

Chestnuts, shelled to reveal the kernel.

Chestnuts, shelled and peeled ready for use.

Coconut, creamed where coconut flesh is cooked and processed into blocks for use as a flavouring.

Coconut, desiccated (U.S. shredded) The dried and grated kernel of the coconut.

Coconut flakes Dried coconut rolled or shredded into flakes.

Coconut flesh or kernel which can be eaten fresh or cooked.

Coconut, long-thread Dried kernel processed into long-threads for a decoration or garnish.

Coconut in shell The fruit of the coconut palm. Consisting of the outer fibrous husk, white flesh and coconut milk.

Hazelnuts in shell Members of the same corylus family of trees including filberts and cob nuts.

Hazelnuts, shelled to reveal the brown-skinned round kernel.

Linseeds Seeds of the flax plant. Principally used now for their oil.

Peanuts in shell Also called groundnuts. Two kernels grow in each nut, which has a soft, cardboard-like shell.

Peanuts, shelled to reveal the kernels complete with pinkish skin.

Peanuts, shelled and peeled by blanching to produce creamy white kernels.

Pecans in shell Smooth, oblong, thin-shelled nuts, native to southern U.S.A.

Pecans, shelled Pecan nuts resemble walnuts.

Pecan halves Pecan kernels separated into halves for mainly dessert use.

Pistachio nuts in shell A nut about the size of a small olive whose shell is cracked for easy separation from the kernel.

Pistachio nuts, shelled to reveal the small bright green kernel.

Pine nuts The seeds of the stone pine. Only available in Britain shelled.

Pumpkin seeds Olive green seeds from the pumpkin.

Sesame seeds Seeds from the sesame plant rich in vitamins and minerals. Ground to a paste, it is used to make tahini.

Sunflower seeds Delicious seeds rich in B complex vitamins, protein, vitamin E and many minerals. Useful as a snack item or to add to salads.

Walnuts in shell The fruit of the walnut tree. Like most nuts, the walnut has a green smooth outer husk which is removed prior to selling, revealing the characteristic wrinkled and gnarled inner shell.

Walnuts, shelled where the outer shell has been cracked to reveal the walnut kernel halves joined together.

Walnut halves where the kernels have been separated into halves.

Almonds in shell

Almonds, shelled

Almonds, blanched

Almonds, slivered

Walnuts in shell

Walnuts, shelled

Walnuts, shelled and halved

Pecans in shell

Pecans, shelled

Pecans, shelled and halved

Hazelnuts in shell

Hazelnuts, shelled

Pine nuts

Pistachio nuts in shell

Pistachio nuts, shelled

Linseeds

Coconut in shell

Long-thread coconut

Coconut flakes/shreds

Coconut, shelled

Desiccated coconut

Creamed coconut

Chestnuts in shell

Chestnuts, shelled

Brazil nuts in shell

Brazil nuts, shelled

Chestnuts, shelled and peeled

Cashew nuts, shelled

Peanuts in shell

Peanuts, shelled

Peanuts, shelled and peeled

Pumpkin seeds

Sunflower seeds

Sesame seeds

Dried bananas

Dried figs

Dried pears

Dried apricots

Dried peaches

Dried apples

Dried dates

Prunes

Muscatel raisins

Currants

Sultanas

Raisins

Dried fruits

Apples, dried Usually peeled, cored and cut into rings, apples when dried still retain all their vitamin C. Many undergo a sulphur treatment to keep the flesh white.

Apricots, dried Plump sun-dried apricots are often preferable to the fresh original since they contain all the goodness of the fresh fruit in a sweetened concentrated form. Particularly valuable to vegetarians for their protein content.

Bananas, dried Fully ripe, high sugar bananas dry superbly well if split lengthwise and dried in the sun. Drying heightens the flavour making it a delicious chewy sweetmeat as well as tasty addition for cakes, cereals and fruit salads.

Currants These are the dried fruit of the tiny, purple Corinth grape, smallest of all the dried fruits, they have a tart flavour and hardish, crisp skin. Also rich in iron and potassium.

Dates, dried Sold dried singly or pressed in blocks, dates dry beautifully due to their high sugar content. Use in making cakes, biscuits (U.S. cookies), pastries and puddings or as a sweetmeat.

Figs, dried Thin-skinned fresh figs do not travel well but this presents little problem if they are sun dried first, resulting in sugar deposits on the skin surface – a sure sign of good quality. Eat raw, re-constitute for use or simply chop to use in baking.

Fruits, candied Not just dried but syrup soaked over time then dried, candied fruits are often used with dried fruit mixtures in baking and dessert making. The vast selection available will include crystallized and candied oranges, pineapple, peaches, pears, nectarines, cherries, citrus fruit peels, kumquats and, of course, not a fruit but nut, glacé chestnuts, called marrons glacés. (Not photographed.)

Fruit mixtures, dried Manufacturers and retailers also offer a good range of mixed dried fruit selections that are worth considering if baking, making a fruit salad or breakfast cereal or muesli mixture.

A basic popular dried fruit mixture will generally include raisins, sultanas (U.S. golden raisins), currants and chopped mixed peel. This is a good basic mixture for use in making rich fruit cakes, biscuits (U.S. cookies) and other baked items.

A dried fruit salad mixture will almost invariably contain dried apricots, peaches, prunes, apples, pears and possibly figs. As a general guideline, the more expensive the mix the more exotic will be the ingredients. (Not photographed.)

Ginger, crystallized Again not a dried fruit but another sweetmeat that is often used with dried fruit mixtures. Here root ginger is peeled then soaked in a sugar syrup. It is then dried and finished with a sugar coating. Use as a decoration, flavouring ingredient or item for a dried fruit salad. (Not photographed.)

Peaches, dried Halved and dried either naturally by the sun or artificially, dried peaches contain an astonishing amount of iron.

Pears, dried Pears are not peeled before drying and so have a characteristic wrinkled outer skin. Many varieties are now becoming available, some being preserved in syrup before drying.

Prunes Prunes are made from plums with a high sugar content, which can be dried without removing the stone (U.S. pit). They have only about half as much sugar as dates, figs or raisins so are valuable dried fruit for the slimmer.

Raisins The most popular of all dried fruits, raisins are dried in the sun or artificially by heat. They are a popular ingredient of dried fruit mixtures for salads and for cake making.

Raisins, muscatel Large, sun-dried plump raisins dried from muscat grapes, more robust than sultanas (U.S. golden raisins) and chewier than currants. Add to muesli (U.S. granola), cakes, biscuits (U.S. cookies), pastries, stuffings, rice mixtures, puddings and salads.

Sultanas (U.S. golden raisins) The dried fruit of the white, seedless sultana grape. Larger and sweeter than raisins and currants, they are prized for their dessert and baking use.

Dried beans

Aduki beans Very small red beans with a sweet nutty taste. Usually soaked and boiled for use or pounded into a fine paste and made into cakes. Aduki beans make a delicious addition to soups, stews, salads and rice dishes.

Beansprouts Commercially grown for sale, these are usually the sprouts of the mung bean although almost any bean can be sprouted. Use in salads, sandwiches and stir-fry dishes. (Not photographed.)

Black beans Shiny black beans that are cooked whole for soups, stews and savoury dishes but mainly used for sprouting.

Black-eye beans White-rounded beans, distinguished by a black mark like an eye on one side. They are used in soups, salads, rice dishes and casseroles. In Africa the dried seeds are ground to make a coffee substitute. The tender immature pods can also be eaten as a vegetable and the developing sprouts are eaten like spinach.

Black fermented Chinese beans These wrinkled looking black beans are usually soya beans preserved in salt. They are very popular in Chinese meat and vegetable dishes. (Not photographed.)

Broad beans Very large, flat, brown beans that are also known as haba, horse or Windsor beans. They are good in vegetable casseroles and hot-pots.

Butter or lima beans Also known as sieva beans, curry beans or pole beans. Lima beans tend to be smaller than the large flat butter bean and have a sweeter taste. Very popular in Britain as an accompanying vegetable.

Cannellini beans Creamy-white kidney beans very popular in Italy. Cooked they have a light almost fluffy texture.

Flageolet beans Pale green beans, long and thin in shape. They are good cooked and puréed, as in pease pudding.

Ful medame beans Small, brown, dull-looking beans with thick skins and earthy taste. Delicious in soups and stews.

Haricot beans The most popular bean of all and used in Boston baked beans. Also known as white haricots and navy beans.

Lablab beans Also called the hyacinth bean. This is a black bean that must be shelled before cooking. Occasionally it is also called the Egyptian bean since it is very popular in the Middle East. (Not photographed.)

Large white beans These are large, white, flat beans of the haricot (U.S. navy) variety. Looking rather like a pale version of broad beans they make delicious ingredients for stews and casseroles. (Not photographed.)

Mung beans Also known as the green gram, golden gram, black gram or Oregon pea, they are the most popular of the sprouting beans. Ranging in colour from green through yellow to golden and black, it is the olive green variety that is generally used for sprouting and cooking.

Pinto beans A variety of haricot bean (U.S. navy bean) with a mottled brown or speckled appearance that changes colour to pink when cooked.

Quick dried green beans These are fresh green beans that have been freeze-dried quickly for preservation. This method ensures a good colour to the beans and quick rehydration for use. They make a good store-cupboard standby for a vegetable at short notice. (Not photographed.)

Red kidney beans Plump, red and shiny these are the beans used in the classic chilli con carne. Also delicious in salads.

Rice beans These small capsule-like dark red/brown beans are so called because of their rice-like taste and shape. Native to China and South East Asia, they are rarely exported to Britain. (Not photographed.)

Rose cocoa or borlotti beans Longish, pink beans with dark flecks that have a noticeable sweet taste. They are delicious cooked with apple in both savoury and sweet mixtures.

Soya beans Nutritiously the most superior of all the beans since they contain complete protein, iron and many vitamins. There are two main types, the edible vegetable bean and commercial field bean which is used to make oil and flour.

Urd beans Also known as the black gram bean, this is found in several different forms but mainly as a cream and black bean smaller than the mung bean. (Not photographed.)

Mung beans

Aduki beans

Soya beans

Haricot beans

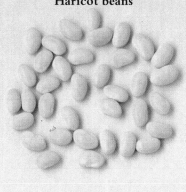

Flageolet beans

Pinto beans

Black beans

Cannellini beans

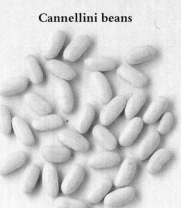

Red kidney beans

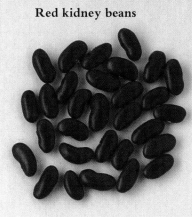

Rose cocoa or borlotti beans

Ful medame beans

Black-eye beans

Butter or lima beans

Broad beans

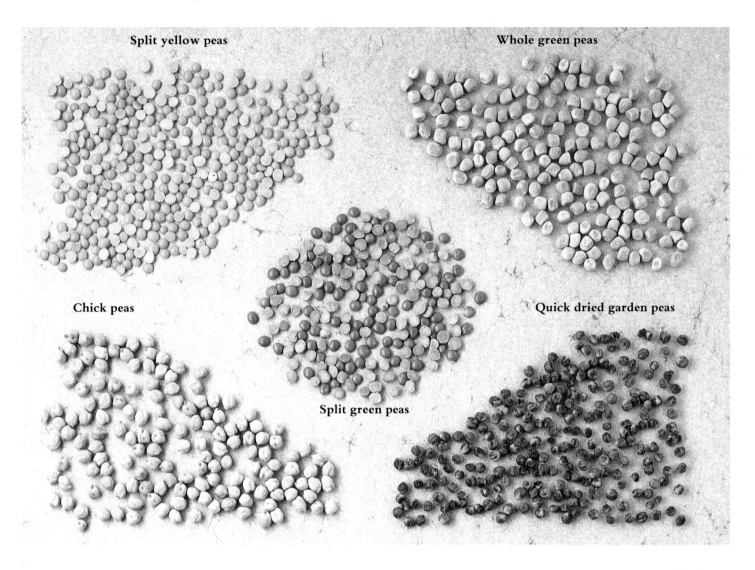

Split yellow peas

Whole green peas

Chick peas

Quick dried garden peas

Split green peas

Dried peas

Blue peas These are whole green peas that have a dark blue-green appearance. They have a very floury texture when cooked and are therefore often used for pea purées. (Not photographed.)

Chick peas Corn-coloured peas also known as garbanzo peas, Bengal grams or Egyptian peas. They can also be white, brown, red or black. They have a distinctive earthy flavour and are used in the classic couscous and hummous.

Garden peas, quick dried Garden peas that have been freeze-dried quickly for preservation. This method retains colour and flavour yet enables peas to rehydrate quickly.

Pigeon peas Not a pea really but a bean also called the gunga pea or toor dal. They are called peas because of their round pea-like shape. Creamy-white and brown they are native to India and the Caribbean where they are eaten in spicy dishes. (Not photographed.)

Split chick peas These are chick peas that have been skinned and then split before cooking. Such treatment ensures a speedier cooking time. (Not photographed.)

Split green peas Very much like split yellow peas except in colour. They are a favourite pea to cook and purée for eating.

Split yellow peas Also called split yellow dhal peas they are usually cooked to make a vegetable purée.

Whole green peas These have a dried pale green wrinkled skin. They are used as a vegetable, in stews, hot-pots and savoury dishes.

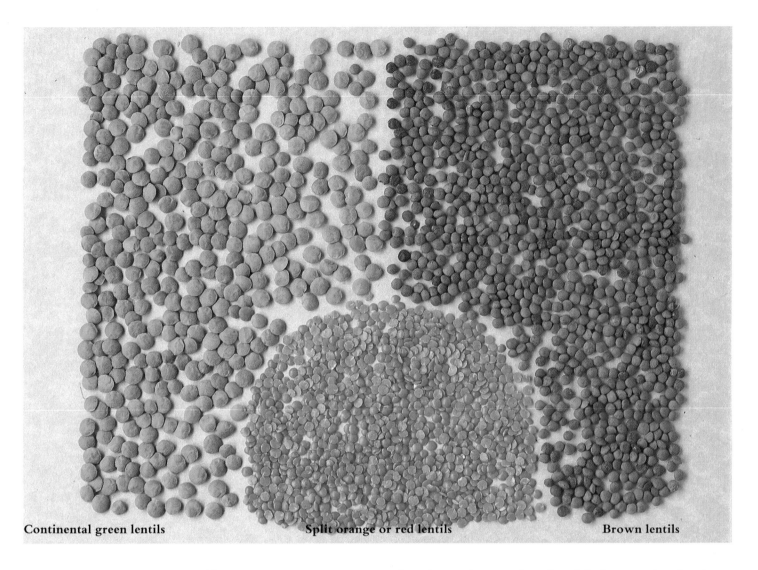

Continental green lentils   **Split orange or red lentils**   **Brown lentils**

Lentils

Lentils are leguminous seeds that vary in colour from white to green, orange, pink and brown. They are a valuable ingredient in vegetarian-style eating for their protein value which exceeds most pulses, save the soya bean. The two main types are Chinese and Indian lentils. Chinese are invariably white to green and Indian vary in shade from pink to brown.

Brown lentils Whole small greeny brown lentils also known as Indian lentils. After a short soaking time they cook to a purée.

Continental green lentils Whole green lentils, about half the size of a pea. Rich in protein, they are tasty in casseroles, stews, vegetable type rissoles and patties, as well as thick, healthy soups. Soak, if liked, before cooking.

Split orange or red lentils The most popular lentil also called the Egyptian lentil. This lentil does not require soaking prior to cooking.

23

Seasonings, flavourings and thickenings

Agar flakes Agar in a quick dissolving popular form as flakes.

Agar powder A product of several sea vegetables valuable for its jelling properties. Used by vegetarians as a replacement for animal gelatine. Use 2 teaspoons agar powder to set 600 ml/1 pint (u.s. 2½ cups) liquid.

Brewer's yeast A by-product of the brewing process, it has outstanding nutritional value. It is rich in proteins and the B vitamins. Use in cereals, crunchy toppings, soups, gravies and casseroles.

Gomashio or sesame salt. This Japanese product is sometimes difficult to locate but a good version can be made by grinding 4 parts roasted sesame seeds with 1 portion salt. Use as a replacement for salt.

Miso A fermented soya bean flavouring or seasoning in spoonable form. Ranging in colour from light brown to almost black, the lighter versions contain less salt.

Salt, sea or crystal salt is obtained by evaporating sea salt in enclosed areas. It is often prized because of its high iodine content.

Salt substitute Low-sodium salt intended for those who wish to cut down on a high intake for medical reasons.

Salt, table Usually salt produced by pumping water into underground salt mines then vacuum drying the resulting brine. Additives like starch, phosphate or lime and potassium may have been added.

Tahini A speciality of the Middle East made from sesame seeds ground to a paste. It can be mixed with lentil purée and oil to make a delicious dip.

Tamari A naturally fermented sauce from the soya bean not unlike but not the same as soya sauce. Gluten-free, this by-product of making miso, is invaluable for special wheat-free diets.

Vegetable concentrates Rather like stock cubes (u.s. bouillon cubes) but in a spoonable form. They can be used like yeast extract to make delicious drinks, stocks and a tasty spread.

Vegetable stock cubes (u.s. vegetable bouillon cubes) Cubes of concentrated vegetables, yeast and flavourings that offer a quick and easy way of making stock.

Yeast extract The soluble residue that is produced when fresh brewer's yeast is mixed with salt then evaporated under pressure. Rich in vitamin B, many vegetarian yeast extracts also contain vegetable protein and iron. They make delicious drinks, stocks and spreads but many have a high salt content so should be taken in moderation.

Vegetable concentrates

Tahini

Miso

Yeast extract

Tamari

Sea salt

Table salt

Agar powder

Brewer's yeast

Agar flakes

Gomashio (sesame salt)

Salt substitute

Vegetable stock cubes

Sweeteners

Carob powder A flavouring from the pulp of the carob or locust bean that has a flavour similar to chocolate. When substituting carob for cocoa powder use only half as much.

Corn syrup or glucose syrup made by heating water and cornstarch with acid.

Honey, clear Nectar from the flowers of plants and trees produced by bees. The composition and flavour depending upon the flowers, the weather, the season and other variations of nature. It can replace sugar in most recipes but only use three-quarters of the amount and reduce the liquid slightly.

Honey, creamed or set Honey that has a proportion of beeswax in it.

Malt extract A syrup that is less sweet than sugar. Use to make malt loaf, cake and a flavoursome malt drink.

Maple syrup Obtained by tapping sugar from the maple tree then boiling and refining. Very sweet and concentrated, it should be used sparingly.

Molasses Also known as blackstrap molasses, is a by-product or end-product of the sugar refining industry. It is rich in vitamins, iron, copper, phosphorus and potassium. Use in milk shakes or as a substitute for honey in all cake, milk and bread recipes.

Sugar, demerara A raw brown sugar that has been only partially refined by cleaning.

Sugar, muscovado A dark brown, moist distinctively flavoured sugar that has been only partially refined.

Sugar, soft dark brown A partially refined sugar with cane molasses added – but check, it can simply be white sugar dyed.

Sugar, soft light brown Another version of the above but lighter in colour.

Molasses · Clear honey · Creamed or set honey · Corn syrup · Soft light brown sugar · Malt extract · Maple syrup · Soft dark brown sugar · Muscovado sugar · Carob powder · Demerara sugar

Gouda

Cheddar

Feta

Ricotta

Hard goat's cheese

Curd cheese

Munster

Cream cheese

Double Gloucester

Vegetable suet

Solid vegetable fat

Yogurt

Chévre

Tofu

Vegetarian cheese

Vegetable ghee

Soya milk

Cottage cheese

Dairy produce and alternatives

It is often very difficult to ascertain whether a cheese is suitable for vegetarian eating or not – i.e. whether it is made with animal rennet. Many cheeses are naturally made without the use of animal rennet and yet others are available both with animal rennet and without. Many vegetarians do not make the distinction and eat all cheeses regardless of rennet used, and certainly within the recipes of this book cheese has been used for flavour and variety rather than for strict vegetarian principles. Listed below, however, are the cheeses that are principally made without animal rennet for information – it may still be essential to ask your retailer for assurance.

Regardless of cheese it will still be important to choose a cheese that is ripe – that is not too dry, too hard, too soft or 'sweaty'. Cracks in hard cheeses are a sure sign of old age, as indeed a very high odour and extremely running texture are of soft cheese varieties. To ensure freshness at home, only buy the amount of cheese you are likely to consume in a week at any one time – and store in a cool larder or refrigerator.

Remove cheeses from the larder or refrigerator about 1 hour before you intend to use or eat them. If you are only going to use a small piece, cut away that piece from the whole and leave to stand rather than 'mature' the whole piece.

Perhaps the greatest disappointment with cheese purchases comes from the softer cheese varieties – what looks like a ripe soft cheese in the chill cabinet can often be dry and chalky at home. Look for a cheese that is soft right through to the middle or centre of the cheese for perfect flavour and texture – a cheese with a chalky white line through it will invariably be under-ripe.

Again store soft cheeses in the larder or refrigerator (the former being the better option) and remove from the refrigerator or larder about 1–2 hours before serving.

Cheese, Cheddar A hard cheese with a smooth, even texture that can be mild and creamy tasting or mature and strong. Made without the addition of animal rennet.
Cheese, Chèvre A French goat's cheese with soft texture that is suitable for vegetarians.
Cheese, cottage A low fat curd cheese made from skimmed milk.
Cheese, cream A soft high fat cheese made from full cream milk.
Cheese, curd A soft cheese made from full cream milk that is set using acid.
Cheese, Double Gloucester A reddish cheese with rich full taste, smooth creamy texture and fine flavour made without animal rennet.
Cheese, Feta A Greek sheep or goat's milk cheese curdled naturally without the use of animal rennet.
Cheese, Gouda A Dutch cheese similar to Edam that is made without animal rennet.
Cheese, hard goat's An animal rennet-free cheese made from goat's milk.
Cheese, Munster A cow's milk cheese made in France and Germany that is made without animal rennet.
Cheese, Ricotta A low fat soft cheese made from whey that is suitable for vegetarians.
Cheese, vegetarian Hard cheese specially made for vegetarians without any animal rennet.
Fat, solid vegetable The vegetarian alternative to lard made from hydrogenated vegetable oils.
Ghee, vegetable A hydrogenated vegetable oil version of the usual popular clarified butter.
Milk, soya A good vegetarian substitute for dairy or cow's milk.
Suet, vegetable A vegetarian suet made from palm nut oil.
Tofu A fermented soya bean curd with a soft, delicate texture and pale colour. It is slightly thicker than cottage cheese and can be used instead of in many recipes.
Yogurt Milk which has been soured with a special culture. To make your own, see page 33.

Equipment

Vegetarian cooking isn't really specialist cooking so it doesn't require any unusual kitchen equipment for its preparation and cooking. There are however a few items that will prove invaluable in any well-equipped kitchen geared to speedy and efficient food preparation and so are worthy of consideration:

Knives A good selection of sharp knives will prove indispensable for slicing, chopping and dicing a multitude of foods. As a basic start have a large knife suitable for slicing bread, a medium-sized knife for cutting pastry and cheese, and a small paring knife for fruit and vegetable preparation.

Scissors A good pair of kitchen scissors will prove useful for snipping herbs and trimming or cutting many foods.

Chopping board A good quality chopping board is essential to protect both work surfaces and knives from undue wear and tear. A wooden one is a good all-purpose option but must be scrubbed thoroughly after use. New strengthened glass boards are becoming popular and are very easy to wipe clean.

Grater Grating, slicing, dicing and mincing are all preparation techniques called upon to introduce variety in vegetable, fruit and dairy produce preparation for vegetarians. For this reason it is worth investing in a good, easy-to-grip, stable box grater to make the grating chore a pleasurable and safe one. If you have a food processor then a grating disc will be provided as a standard but you may wish to consider buying a supplementary fine or coarse disc in addition to the medium.

Saucepans Good quality saucepans will provide years of excellent use so consider and weigh-up carefully the attributes of the many ranges currently available. Always choose the very best you can afford remembering that those with thick heavy bases ensure a good uniform cooking and heat distribution to the pan contents.

Pressure cooker Alongside your normal range of pans, you may wish to invest in a pressure cooker for speedy cooking of beans, vegetables, grains and fruits. For versatility choose a model with variable pressure controls (high, medium and low or 7 kg/15 lb, 4.5 kg/10 lb and 2.25 kg/5 lb pressure).

Scales Scales are an absolute must to make sure that ingredients are calculated in the correct proportions. For the same reason *measuring spoons* and *measuring jugs* are vital.

Sieves Many ingredients need to be sifted before use or sieved and puréed after cooking so a nylon or metal sieve will prove invaluable. If you do not have a blender or food processor then a *vegetable mill* in addition to a sieve may seem a worthwhile buy for puréeing soups and vegetables.

Food blender/processor The new kitchen wizards enabling speedy chopping, slicing, grating, puréeing, mincing, mixing and kneading depending upon the machine and model. If you are an enthusiastic bread maker then look for a model with kneading action or a dough hook.

Most basic food processors come with a grating, slicing and metal blade as standards – all are useful attachments which are required in vegetarian food preparation.

Rolling-pin A rolling-pin will be essential if you intend to make pastry for pies, desserts, savoury quiches and flans. Choose a rolling-pin that is long, even and without any ridges. The majority of cooks choose a wooden one but today there are also a vast number of so-called cool pins available. These are hollow rolling-pins that can be filled with cold water – ensuring that the pastry stays cool during handling. Others are made of marble for coolness and yet others from strengthened glass.

Your rolling-pin will have many other essential uses – it will help to crush biscuits (U.S. cookies), crackers and other savoury baked items for coatings and crumbs for cheesecake bases and other savoury dishes and help to shape breads and biscuits prior to baking.

Baking beans It is essential to weigh down pastry cases during any blind baking and baking beans are usually the item requested for success. You can buy special ceramic or china baking beans for the purpose but it is just as easy to gather a jar full of end of bean packets for the same use. They can be used over and over again, so once collected they will have many years of use.

Freezing and storing

It is often economical on time, effort, energy and money to buy and prepare food in bulk. Many foods will keep well in the storecupboard and refrigerator, and many will freeze successfully. Consult the chart below for precise times and instructions:

Food	Storage times and instructions
Fruit	
fresh	use as soon as possible after purchase or harvesting *or* freeze (consult your freezer handbook for precise instructions) for 3–12 months.
dried	store in a cool dry airtight container for up to 6 months *or* freeze for up to 1 year.
Nuts and seeds	
unshelled	store in a cool dry place for up to 6 months.
shelled	store in an airtight tin or container for up to 3 months.
chopped or ground	store in an airtight container for up to 6 weeks.
Seasonings	
gomashio	use within 2 weeks.
dried herbs	store in a cool, dry and dark place for up to 4 months.
Sweeteners	
brown sugar	store in an airtight jar for up to 6 months.
honey	store almost indefinitely. If the honey crystallizes then warm to clear.
Sea vegetables	
packaged (cleaned and dried)	once opened store in a dry place for up to 4 months.

Food	Storage times and instructions
Vegetables	
fresh	use as soon as possible after purchase or harvesting *or* freeze (consult your freezer handbook for precise instructions) for 3–9 months.
sprouts, bean	store in the refrigerator for up to 4–5 days. *Do not freeze.*
dried	store in an airtight container for up to 1 year.
Peas, beans and lentils	
raw	store in a cool dry place for up to 1 year.
cooked	store covered in the refrigerator for 2–3 days *or* open freeze then bag and freeze for up to 3 months.
Dairy produce	
oils	keep in a cool dark place for up to 2 months.
butter, margarine, spreads and ghee	store in the refrigerator for up to 2 weeks *or* freeze for up to 2 months.
tofu	keep loose tofu in the refrigerator under water (change daily) for up to 1 week. Vacuum packed tofu will keep unopened for 3–4 weeks.
eggs	store in the refrigerator for up to 3 weeks *or* freeze, ideally separated, for up to 3 months.

Cooking and growing techniques

Vegetarian cooking does not involve any special cooking techniques, although there will be some which will be called into practise more often than others. Perfectly cooked separate rice, 'al dente' pasta, crisp yet tender vegetables and properly cooked dried beans can be the make or break of a meal so it is important to get them right.

Cooking long-grain rice

For basic cooking of long-grain rice, allow 2 teacups long-grain rice for four people. Place 4 teacups water in a pan with $\frac{1}{2}$ teaspoon salt. Bring to the boil, add the rice and stir well. Bring to the boil again, reduce the heat, cover and simmer until tender. By the end of the cooking time the rice grains will have absorbed the liquid and be fluffy and separate. White rice will take about 15 minutes cooking time and brown rice about 25–30 minutes.

If the rice is of the American easy-cook or par-boiled variety then use 5 teacups water to 2 teacups rice and cook for about 20 minutes.

Cooking pasta

For basic cooking of pasta, allow 50 g/2 oz (U.S. $\frac{1}{2}$ cup) dried pasta per person. Cook each 100 g/4 oz (U.S. 1 cup) pasta in at least 1.2 litres/2 pints (U.S. 5 cups) water.

Place the water and salt to taste in a pan and bring to the boil. Add the pasta, stir briskly, bring to the boil and cook for the time stated on the packet instructions, about 8–15 minutes. Drain and serve.

Cooking times for dried pasta often depend upon the size and shape of the pasta. There are many different varieties on sale – including green pasta (usually spinach flavoured), yellow pasta (egg enriched) and red pasta (tomato flavoured). Shapes are numerous and it is said that there is a different shape on sale in Italy for every day of the year! Popular varieties and shapes sold here include:

Penne A pasta shape that looks like a pen quill.

Bows A pasta shape that looks like a small crinkled bow.

Wagon wheel A small wheel-like pasta shape.

Twistetti Curly twists of pasta cut into short lengths.

Elbow macaroni Quarter moons of hollow pasta shaped rather like a bent elbow.

Fettucini A folded nest of ribbon fine noodles that unfold when cooked.

Rings Fine rings of pasta that cook extra fast.

Shells A pasta shape that looks like a small shell.

Basic vegetable cooking

Cooking instructions of vegetables vary enormously depending upon their preparation, age, end-use and size. Perhaps the most critical cooking and timing is when serving vegetables at their simplest – boiled.

For boiling vegetables, bring the water to the boil, add a little salt and the vegetables. Cook for the recommended times given below, remembering to use only the minimum amount of water (just enough to cover):

Vegetables	Cooking time (minutes)
asparagus spears	15–20
beans, broad (U.S. fava or lima)	10–15
French	5–10
runner (U.S. green)	10–15
beetroot (U.S. beet)	40–60
broccoli	10–12
Brussels sprouts	6–8
cabbage and greens	3–6
carrots	10–15
cauliflower florets	8–10
celeriac and kohlrabi	10–15
celery	10–15
corn-on-the-cob	10–12
courgettes (U.S. zucchini)	6–8
fennel	10–15
leeks	10–15
mangetout (U.S. snow peas)	3–5
okra	15–20
onions, sliced	5
parsnips, sliced	15
peas	8–12
potatoes, old	20–25
new	20–25
salsify	20–30
spinach	8–10
swede (U.S. rutabaga)	30
turnips, chopped	15–20

To sprout beans

Beansprouts are endlessly versatile ingredients to add to salads, vegetable stir-fry mixtures, sandwich fillings and Chinese style dishes. Almost any bean or grain can be sprouted but remember grain sprouts take about 3 days to sprout whereas beans and lentils need 4–7 days.

Mung beans, aduki beans, alfalfa and whole lentils are popular and easy to sprout.

To sprout mung beans

Wash the beans thoroughly. Place 2 tablespoons into a wide-necked jar and fill up with lukewarm water. Leave to stand overnight.

Drain off the water, cover the jar with muslin (U.S. cheesecloth) and an elastic band. Leave the jar upside-down to drain in a warm place (an airing cupboard is ideal).

Every night and morning, until the sprouts are ready, rinse the beans in the jar with lukewarm water. Shake gently then drain thoroughly. Turn upside-down again to drain.

The sprouts will be ready in about 4 days by which time they will have grown to about 4–5 cm/1½–2 inches in length. Carefully remove from the jar and rinse before using.

31

Cooking dried peas, beans, grains and lentils

Food	Preparation	Average cooking time (minutes)
aduki beans	soak overnight	45
barley	toast if liked. Cook 1 cup grain in 4 cups liquid	50–60
black-eye beans	soak overnight	45–50
black beans	soak overnight	50–60
broad beans (U.S. lima or fava)	soak overnight	90
buckwheat	toast if liked. Cook 1 cup grain in $2\frac{1}{2}$ cups liquid	20
butter beans (U.S. lima beans)	soak overnight	60–90
cannellini beans	soak overnight	45–50
chick peas (U.S. garbanzo)	soak overnight	60–90
flageolet beans	soak overnight	45–50
Ful medame beans	soak overnight	55–60
green peas, whole	soak overnight	60–90
haricot beans (U.S. navy)	soak overnight	50–60
lentils, whole	do not soak	30–45
split	do not soak	15–30
millet	toast if liked. Cook 1 cup grain in $2\frac{1}{2}$–3 cups liquid	20
mung beans	soak if liked	30–45
peas, whole	soak overnight	60–90
split	do not soak	40–45
pinto beans	soak overnight	60–90
red kidney beans	soak overnight	45–50
rye	soak overnight. Cook 1 cup grain in 3 cups liquid	50–60
soya beans	soak overnight	$2\frac{1}{4}$–$2\frac{1}{2}$ hours
wheat	soak overnight. Cook 1 cup grain in 4 cups liquid	50–60

Growing and preparation techniques

Some ingredients and foods are called upon frequently in vegetarian cooking and it is important that they are young, fresh and in prime condition. One of the simplest ways of ensuring this is to grow or prepare your own. Freshly-sprouted beans, freshly made yogurt and rich cream cheese have endless versatile uses and are worth the trouble of making at home.

To make soft yogurt cheese

A soft cream-like cheese is ideal for adding to main-course dishes but is delicious served simply with crackers, crispbreads or freshly-baked bread. If liked roll the cheese in chopped herbs, nuts or sesame seeds before serving:

Line a colander or strainer with muslin (U.S. cheese-cloth) and stand over a bowl. Add 600 ml/1 pint (U.S. $2\frac{1}{2}$ cups) yogurt and tie with string to form a bag. Lift out of the colander and tie the strings to a tap over a sink to drain overnight.

The following day, tip the curds from the muslin into a bowl and beat until smooth. Add salt and pepper to taste and 2 teaspoons olive oil, blending well. Form into a flat, round shape and coat in herbs, nuts or seeds as liked. Chill thoroughly before serving. **Serves 4**

To dry herbs

A good supply of dried herbs can lift an ordinary dish into the luxury class. Pick in early mid-summer just before they flower, on a dry day, in the morning after the dew has evaporated.

Carefully pick off any damaged leaves and rinse, if necessary, in cold water.

Tie freshly picked herbs into small bunches and dip briefly into boiling water – about $\frac{1}{2}$–1 minute. Shake well and leave to drain on absorbent kitchen towel.

Place on muslin-lined (U.S. cheesecloth-lined) metal racks or into brown paper bags. Place or hang in an airing cupboard and leave to dry for 3–5 days.

If liked, the herbs can be stripped from their stems for storage. Crumble lightly after drying and store in air-tight jars or pots in a cool, dry place out of direct sunlight.

Yogurt

Yogurt, to many people, and to many cultures, has an almost spiritual value – it is associated with longevity and fertility in many countries and features prominently in many of their classical dishes.

According to an ancient tradition it is said that an angel revealed to the prophet Abraham the secret method of making yogurt – a secret that has been passed on and varies little to the modern day production methods now employed by many modern manufacturers – many varieties sold today differ little from the primitive variety save additives and preservatives that are included to prolong shelf life.

The glowing testimonial that yogurt receives however is less certain to prove and many claim properties of this simple food that are almost impossible to meet. It is known however that yogurt does produce an environment in the intestine that is unfavourable to harmful bacteria – so taken on a regular basis probably has a great deal of value to general good health. The claims for fertility range far and wide and must be treated with some scepticism – although the Bible does tell us that Abraham, perhaps the founder of yogurt, lived to 175 and fathered a child at 100!

Suffice to say yogurt is a valued food and has a place within the modern vegetarian diet – here is a quick, easy and almost foolproof way of making natural yogurt at home without the use of preservatives and other additives.

To make natural yogurt

Bring 600 ml/1 pint (U.S. 2½ cups) milk to the boil and hold for about 5 seconds. Let it cool down to 43°C/110°F, just above body temperature, so that it feels comfortable when tested with a clean finger.

Pour the milk into a flask. Stir in 2 tablespoons live yogurt. Screw the top on the flask and leave to thicken. This will take about 3–8 hours.

Refrigerate as soon as thickened but do not shake as this causes curds to form. Mix with honey or fruit for extra flavour if liked.

Alternatively use an electric yogurt maker, complete with thermostatically controlled temperature gauge and serving pots, according to the manufacturer's instructions.

Menu planning

It is often a frequent criticism of vegetarian food that it is difficult to know what to serve with what. No so difficult with meat and two vegetables but when it is meat-free, more complex.

It certainly is a question of familiarity and in time it seems simple to plan an exotic dinner party, children's party menu or simple carefree lunch the vegetarian way.

Practicalities to consider include texture, flavour, colour and convenience but it is also important to consider dietary or nutritional requirements. Balance light starters and main courses with heartier puddings; or satisfying nibbles and a main course feast with a light dessert offering. Weigh main course 'anchors' like rice, pasta, potatoes and other grains or cereals with lighter vegetables, fruits, nuts, seeds and dairy produce – remembering at all times that variety is all-important.

But most of all don't make vegetarian eating a chore – use your refrigerator and freezer to full effect in preparing dishes in advance or in bulk – especially the time-costly ones and rely upon the odd one or two convenience foods to speed up a dish (but check the list of ingredients).

The following menus have been planned with these considerations in mind and should provide a good starting point and springboard for your own ideas.

Suggested menus

Christmas Dinner Menu
Apple and Chestnut Soup (page 48)
Lasagne with Courgettes and Corn (page 176)
or Red Cabbage Parcels (page 179)
with Vegan Pilaff (page 112)
Orange, Spinach and Mushroom Salad (page 99)
Neapolitan Honey Pudding (page 153)
or Festive Cranberry Flan (page 154)
Blackcurrant Sorbet (page 145)
Chestnut Yule Log (page 188)
Festive Mince Pies (page 186)

Picnic Menu
Pecan and Onion Tart (page 57)
Herb Dressed Cheese Salad (page 76)
Relishes (page 88)
Mushroom Slaw (page 95)
Chilli Beansprouts (page 117)
Pitta Salad Pockets (page 123)
Kishmish (page 154)
or Pineapple Fruit Salad (page 185)
Almond Shortbread Fingers (page 163)

Children's Party Menu
Cheesy Crust Toasties (page 104)
Bean Rafts (page 106)
Crunchy Apple and Cheshire Flan (page 106)
or Herby Vegetable Tart (page 104)
Banana and Honey Ice-cream (page 144)
Energy Wedges (page 108)
or Fruity Orange Slice (page 109)
Carob Cream Cake (page 172)

Buffet Supper Menu
Cheese and Raisin Dip (page 46)
Corny Dippers Delight (page 46)
Stuffed Jacket Potatoes (page 54)
Vegetable Cobbler (page 66)
Green Salad with Tomato and Herb Dressing (page 87)
Strawberry Shortcake (page 184)
Cheese, Celery and Biscuits (u.s. savory crackers)

Summer Informal Lunch Menu
Green Vegetable Herb Pâté (page 51)
Savoury Cheesecake (page 58)
Caesar Bean Salad (page 96)
Beansprout and Corn Toss Up (page 120)
Lime Crème (page 146)
or Fresh Fruit Shells (page 183)

Winter Lunch Menu
Hot Cheese Bits (page 49)
Tuscany Pizza (page 79)
Mushroom Bean Salad (page 99)
Discovery Dessert (page 148)
or Baked Bramleys with Honey, Fruit
and Walnut Filling (page 150)

Slimmer's Three-course Meal
(for under 600 calories per person)
Crunchy Melon Salad (page 139)
Red Bean Bake (page 136)
Baked Sponge Puddings (page 141)
Low-calorie Minerals

Storecupboard Family Meal
Devilled Mushrooms (page 129)
Mixed Bean Casserole (page 130)
or Vegetable and Cheesy Yogurt Lasagne
(page 129)
Pear Upside-down Cake (page 155)
or Scotch Pancakes with Lemon Butter
(page 157)

Special Occasion Dinner
Cream of Mustard Soup (page 177)
Cheese Soda Bread (page 177)
Crunchy Topped Vegetable Soufflé
(page 180)
or Dolmas (page 180) with Rice
Tomato and Mushroom Sauce (page 84)
Crunchy Vegetable Salad (page 117)
Vacherin aux Marrons (page 151)
or Pear Galette (page 168)
Cheese and Crackers

Family Dinner
Old-fashioned Vegetable Soup (page 46)
Wholewheat Bread (page 160)
Vegetarian Lasagne (page 61)
Waldorf Bean Salad (page 97)
or Chick Pea, Corn and Apple Salad
(page 112)
Scotch Pancakes with Lemon Butter
(page 157)

Breakfasts and brunches

Light and sustaining or hearty and satisfying, a breakfast offers a good start to the day. Taken later it can double as a lunch, named brunch, and will ensure that you last the course until dinner or supper time. Carefully balanced for variety, exquisitely arranged and prepared it also makes the perfect entertaining occasion for busy people in a hurry.

The hearty, pan-fried full English breakfast assembly seems to have lost favour, for weekdays at least, but has been replaced with a more convenient and healthy alternative – cereals, fresh fruit, natural yogurt, whole-grain breads and eggs in all their guises. Mixed and matched they offer a daily variety that will never bore – especially if you make your own cereal mixture, fruit salads and nutted, seeded or flavoured breads according to family likes and dislikes or what is in season. Make muesli in bulk for economy of effort and cost, and add luxury items like special dried fruit, toasted nuts, sliced fresh fruit, honey and yogurt to the individual bowl as liked. Or make a chilled breakfast fruit salad using fresh or dried fruits in quantity – it will keep cheerfully in the refrigerator for up to 4 days and will easily double as a dessert in a hurry. Warm and serve with yogurt or cream for breakfast ring the changes.

For some, breakfast is a meal that is hard to warm to – for those a selection of 'meal-in-the-glass' alternatives have been suggested in this section. Undoubtedly they will also appeal to those who take breakfast on the move.

Above left: *Honey juice riser (recipe page 41)*
Left: *Bean stuffed tomatoes (recipe page 43)*
Right: *Crunchy muesli (recipe page 38)*

Early morning breakfast crunch

(Illustrated opposite)

50 g/2 oz (U.S. 2 cups) bran flakes
50 g/2 oz (U.S. ⅓ cup) All Bran or Bran Buds
40 g/1½ oz flaked almonds (U.S. ⅓ cup slivered almonds)
50 g/2 oz (U.S. ⅓ cup) dried apricots, chopped
50 g/2 oz (U.S. ⅓ cup) dried apple, chopped
50 g/2 oz (U.S. ⅓ cup) raisins
milk or natural yogurt to serve

Mix the bran flakes with the All Bran, almonds, apricots, apple and raisins, tossing lightly to mix.

Serve with a little milk or natural yogurt. **Serves 4**

Breakfast fruit compote

(Illustrated opposite)

75 g/3 oz (U.S. ½ cup) dried prunes
75 g/3 oz (U.S. ½ cup) dried apricots
50 g/2 oz (U.S. ⅓ cup) raisins
3 bananas, peeled and thickly sliced
25 g/1 oz (U.S. 1½ tablespoons) clear honey
grated rind of ½ lemon
25 g/1 oz (U.S. 2 tablespoons) butter or margarine
200 ml/7 fl oz (U.S. scant 1 cup) unsweetened orange juice

Soak the prunes and apricots overnight in cold water. Drain and place in an ovenproof dish with the raisins and bananas.

Dissolve the honey in a little warm water and pour over the dried fruit and banana mixture. Sprinkle with the lemon rind and dot with the butter.

Cover and bake in a preheated moderate oven (180 °C, 350 °F, Gas Mark 4) for 35 minutes.

Add the orange juice and return to the oven for a further 5 minutes. Serve warm with a little natural yogurt if liked. **Serves 4**

Crunchy muesli

(Illustrated opposite and on pages 36–37)

225 g/8 oz (U.S. 2⅔ cups) rolled oats
75 g/3 oz (U.S. 6 tablespoons) unrefined demerara or light muscovado sugar
50 g/2 oz (U.S. ½ cup) hazelnuts or almonds, chopped
50 g/2 oz sultanas or raisins (U.S. ⅓ cup golden raisins or raisins)
75 g/3 oz (U.S. ½ cup) dried apricots, chopped

Place the oats, sugar and nuts on a large baking tray, mixing well to blend. Cook under a preheated hot grill (U.S. broiler) until golden, stirring frequently. Allow to cool.

Mix the oat mixture with the sultanas or raisins and apricots, blending well. Store in an airtight tin or container until required.

Serve for breakfast with milk or natural yogurt and sliced fresh fruit in season. **Makes 500 g/18 oz**

Variations

There is no standard or 'approved' recipe for muesli and the choice of ingredients to use is very much a personal one, so for variety and to ring the changes in the above basic, try replacing bran flakes or wheat flakes for the rolled oats; pine kernels, pistachios, walnuts, cashews or Brazil nuts for the hazelnuts or almonds; and dried peaches, nectarines, apples, pears, bananas, figs, dates and currants for the sultanas or raisins and apricots. Serve with milk, cream, soured cream, yogurt, fruit juice or fresh fruit in season as liked.

Above: *Early morning breakfast crunch*
Centre: *Crunchy muesli*
Below: *Breakfast fruit compote*

Apricot get me up

(Illustrated left)

450 ml/$\frac{3}{4}$ pint (U.S. 2 cups) milk
150 ml/$\frac{1}{4}$ pint (U.S. $\frac{2}{3}$ cup) apricot juice or nectar
5 tablespoons (U.S. 6 tablespoons) natural yogurt
orange slices to decorate

Mix the milk with the apricot juice or nectar and yogurt, blending well.
Pour into two large glasses and decorate with orange slices. Serve at once. **Serves 2**

Above left: *Apricot get me up*
Left: *Honey juice riser*
Right: *Corny brunch bread with syrup*

Corny brunch bread

(Illustrated below)

475 ml/16 fl oz (U.S. $2\frac{1}{8}$ cups) milk
100 g/4 oz (U.S. $\frac{3}{4}$ cup) yellow corn meal
1 teaspoon salt
25 g/1 oz (U.S. 2 tablespoons) butter
2 tablespoons (U.S. 3 tablespoons) finely chopped
green pepper
1 × 340 g/12 oz can sweetcorn kernels (U.S. whole
kernel corn), drained
100 g/4 oz (U.S. 1 cup) Cheddar cheese, grated
4 eggs, separated

Heat the milk in a pan to just below boiling point, to
scald. Add the corn meal, salt and butter, stirring well
to blend and melt the butter.

Add the pepper, sweetcorn kernels, cheese and egg
yolks, blending well. Cook over a gentle heat until the
cheese melts. Remove from the heat.

Whisk the egg whites until they stand in stiff peaks.
Fold into the corn mixture with a metal spoon.

Pour into a well greased 28 × 18 × 4 cm/11 × 7 × $1\frac{1}{2}$
inch loaf tin. Bake in a preheated moderate oven (180°C,
350°F, Gas Mark 4) for 45 minutes.

Serve warm in slices with melted butter or maple
syrup. **Serves 8–10**

Honey juice riser

(Illustrated left and on pages 36–37)

1 egg, separated
4 teaspoons clear honey
4 teaspoons wheatgerm
450 ml/$\frac{3}{4}$ pint (U.S. 2 cups) milk, chilled
150 ml/$\frac{1}{4}$ pint (U.S. $\frac{2}{3}$ cup) fruit nectar

Place the egg yolk, honey, wheatgerm, milk and fruit
nectar in a jug. Mix well to blend.

Whisk the egg white until it stands in stiff peaks. Fold
into the milk mixture with a metal spoon.

Pour into cold glasses to serve as a liquid breakfast.
Serves 2

Bean stuffed tomatoes

(Illustrated opposite and on page 36)

4 large tomatoes
salt and freshly ground black pepper
4 small cubes Cheddar cheese
1 × 450 g/1 lb can baked beans in tomato sauce, drained
6 eggs
1 tablespoon cream
40 g/1½ oz (U.S. 3 tablespoons) butter
2 teaspoons snipped chives
4 slices hot buttered wholewheat toast

Cut a thin slice from the top of each tomato, scoop out and discard the seeds. For a fancy finish, cut a zig-zag line around each tomato when removing the top. Season the inner tomato flesh with salt and pepper to taste.

Place a cube of cheese in each tomato and fill with baked beans. Place in a lightly greased ovenproof dish and cover with foil. Bake in a preheated moderately hot oven (200°C, 400°F, Gas Mark 6) for 10–12 minutes.

Meanwhile to make the scrambled egg, beat the eggs with the cream and salt and pepper to taste. Melt the butter in a pan, add the egg mixture and chives and stir gently over a moderate heat until the egg forms thick, creamy flakes.

Cover each slice of buttered toast with the scrambled egg and top with a stuffed tomato. Serve at once.
Serves 4

Egg dipped bread and beans

(Illustrated opposite)

2 eggs
3 tablespoons single cream (U.S. 4 tablespoons light cream)
salt and freshly ground black pepper
12 small flat mushrooms, wiped
oil for frying
2 × 450 g/1 lb cans baked beans in tomato sauce
8 small slices wholewheat bread
75 g/3 oz (U.S. ¾ cup) cheese, grated
parsley or watercress sprigs to garnish

Beat the eggs with the cream and salt and pepper to taste.

Trim the stalks of the mushrooms and brush with a little oil. Grill (U.S. broil) until just cooked, about 4 minutes.

Meanwhile, heat the beans in a pan until hot and bubbly.

Heat about 5 mm/¼ inch oil in a frying pan (skillet). Dip each slice of bread into the beaten egg mixture. Lower carefully into the pan and fry until lightly golden on both sides.

Place the slices of egg fried bread on to the rack of the grill (U.S. broiler) pan. Top with the baked beans and then with the cooked mushrooms.

Sprinkle with cheese and grill for 2 minutes until hot, melted and bubbly. Serve at once. **Serves 4**

Variations
Egg dipped bread and beans can taste doubly delicious if you flavour the basic egg dipping mixture with a variety of ingredients prior to cooking. Try adding 2 teaspoons chopped fresh herbs or 1 teaspoon dried herbs of the mild variety like chives, parsley or chervil; add 2 table-spoons freshly grated mild Cheddar or other vegetarian cheese; 2 teaspoons finely grated onion or snipped spring onion (U.S. scallion) tops; a pinch of mild chilli powder, seasoning salt or flavoured pepper; or 1 teaspoon sesame or other seeds to add flavour, crunch and colour. Other variations include using curried, cassoulet, barbecue or other flavoured beans instead of the basic tomato sauce variety.

Above: *Bean stuffed tomatoes*
Below: *Egg dipped bread and beans*

Soups
and starters

A dip to dunk, a soup to savour or a pâté to spread – whatever your appetizer choice you'll find a recipe to please in this chapter. Light or appetizing; hot or chilled; based on fruit, vegetables, rice or cheese; easy on the pocket or simply luxurious, there is a host of easy to prepare soups and starters to suit any meal whether it be simply family style or exotically entertaining.

Opt for a substantial soup laden with vegetables or a rich creamy-smooth pâté when appetites are large or a main course is light; and serve bite-sized nibbles with a selection of dips or hot mouth-sized savouries like Hot Cheese Bits when a 'teaser' is required to tempt the palate for a man-sized main dish.

Many can be made ahead and refrigerated or frozen to help the busy family cook or hostess but they can appear time-weighty if served with wedges of home-made wholewheat bread, fancy cut-out croûtons or delicately curled Melba toast.

Vegetarian soups and starters rarely pose a problem of choice to the traditional meat-cooking cook but many vegetarians are disappointed when faced with what often appears as yet another mini-sized version of a main course – don't fall into that trap if you're a new vegetarian follower and be adventurous by trying unusual vegetable combinations or presentations for your soup or starter course. Try Apple and Chestnut Soup or Danish Blue Cheesecake for example – both are dishes that are not predictable in terms of flavour, texture and presentation.

Above left: *Old-fashioned vegetable soup (recipe page 46)*
Left: *Savoury stuffed mushrooms (recipe page 49)*
Right: *Corny dippers delight (recipe page 46)*

Fruity rice starter

(Illustrated opposite)

225 g/8 oz (U.S. generous 1 cup) long-grain brown rice
450 ml/¾ pint (U.S. 2 cups) apple juice
450 ml/¾ pint (U.S. 2 cups) water
1 red pepper, cored, seeded and chopped
1 orange, peeled, pith removed, cut into segments
and chopped
4 spring onions (U.S. scallions), trimmed and
chopped
50 g/2 oz (U.S. ⅓ cup) raisins
2 tablespoons chopped fresh parsley
Dressing
2 tablespoons olive oil
1 teaspoon Dijon mustard
1 tablespoon wine vinegar
salt and freshly ground black pepper

Place the rice in a pan with the apple juice and water. Bring to the boil, reduce the heat, cover and simmer until tender and the liquid is absorbed, about 30–40 minutes.

Add the pepper, orange, spring onions, raisins and parsley, blending well.

Place all the dressing ingredients in a screw-topped jar and shake well to mix. Pour over the rice and toss together. Serve warm or cold. **Serves 4–6**

Corny dippers delight

(Illustrated on pages 44–45)

1 × 225 g/8 oz packet cream cheese, softened
75 ml/3 fl oz (U.S. ⅓ cup) soured cream
2 tablespoons finely chopped onion
2 tablespoons snipped chives
2 tablespoons chopped red pepper
2 tablespoons chopped black olives (U.S. ripe olives)
1 tablespoon lemon juice
1 × 340 g/12 oz can sweetcorn kernels (U.S. whole
kernel corn), drained
salt and freshly ground black pepper
crisp savoury crackers or raw vegetable crudités
to serve

Beat the cream cheese with the soured cream until smooth.

Add the onion, chives, pepper, olives, lemon juice, sweetcorn kernels and salt and pepper to taste, blending well. Chill thoroughly.

Serve lightly chilled with crisp savoury crackers or raw vegetable crudités. **Serves 4–6**

Cheese and raisin dip

(Illustrated opposite)

225 g/8 oz (U.S. 1 cup) low fat soft cheese
50 g/2 oz (U.S. ½ cup) Danish Blue or Stilton
cheese, grated
50 g/2 oz (U.S. ⅓ cup) raisins, coarsely chopped
1 teaspoon Worcestershire sauce
2 teaspoons chopped fresh parsley
salt and freshly ground black pepper
raw vegetable crudités to serve

Beat the cheeses together until creamy. Add the raisins, Worcestershire sauce, parsley and salt and pepper to taste, blending well.

Spoon into a small serving bowl and place on a plate. Surround with vegetable crudités for dipping.
Serves 6

Old-fashioned vegetable soup

(Illustrated on pages 44–45)

1 tablespoon oil
175 g/6 oz (U.S. 1 cup) leeks, sliced
1 onion, peeled and chopped
175 g/6 oz (U.S. 1 cup) potatoes, peeled and chopped
175 g/6 oz (U.S. ¾ cup) carrots, peeled and sliced
3–4 stalks celery, scrubbed and sliced
1 × 793 g/1 lb 12 oz can peeled tomatoes
1 litre/1¾ pints (U.S. 4¼ cups) water
salt and freshly ground black pepper
¼ teaspoon dried basil
¼ teaspoon dried thyme
1 bay leaf
1 vegetable stock cube (U.S. 1 vegetable bouillon
cube)
1 × 198 g/7 oz can sweetcorn kernels (U.S. whole
kernel corn), drained
1 × 284 g/10 oz can diagonal-cut green beans, drained
1 × 284 g/10 oz can garden peas, drained

Heat the oil in a large pan. Add the leeks and onion and cook until just golden, about 10 minutes.

Stir in the potatoes, carrots, celery, tomatoes and their juice, water, salt and pepper to taste, basil, thyme, bay leaf and stock cube, blending well.

Bring to the boil, reduce the heat and simmer for 30 minutes or until the vegetables are tender.

Add the sweetcorn kernels, beans and peas. Cook for 5 minutes. Serve with bread. **Serves 8**

Above: Fruity rice starter
Below: Cheese and raisin dip

Apple and chestnut soup

(Illustrated above)

450 g/1 lb chestnuts
1.2 litres/2 pints (U.S. 5 cups) well-flavoured
vegetable stock
½ teaspoon dried mixed herbs
50 g/2 oz (U.S. ¼ cup) butter
2−3 stalks celery, scrubbed and sliced
1 onion, peeled and chopped
450 g/1 lb cooking apples, peeled, cored and sliced
salt and freshly ground black pepper
1−2 tablespoons lemon juice
100 ml/4 fl oz single cream (U.S. ½ cup light cream)
croûtons to garnish

Cut a cross through the shell on one side of the chestnuts and either boil in water for 10 minutes or roast in a hot oven until they split. Remove the outer shells and the inner brown skins.

Place the chestnuts in a pan with the stock and herbs and cook for 20 minutes until tender.

Meanwhile, melt the butter in a pan. Add the celery and onion and cook until softened, about 5−8 minutes. Add the apples and cook until softened, about 5 minutes.

Purée the chestnuts and stock with the apple mixture in a blender, food processor or pass through a fine sieve. Return to the pan and add salt and pepper to taste, the lemon juice and cream, blending well. Reheat gently but do not boil.

Serve hot, sprinkled with crisp croûtons. **Serves 4−6**

Apple and cabbage soup

(Illustrated above and back cover)

50 g/2 oz (U.S. ¼ cup) butter
3 onions, peeled and thinly sliced
675 g/1½ lb cooking apples, peeled, cored and sliced
½ large heart of Savoy cabbage or 450 g/1 lb spring
greens, shredded
1.75 litres/3 pints (U.S. 7½ cups) well-flavoured
vegetable stock
salt and freshly ground black pepper
2−3 tablespoons chopped fresh parsley
parsley sprig to garnish

Melt the butter in a large pan. Add the onion and cook until softened, about 5−8 minutes. Add the apples and cabbage and continue cooking until the cabbage is bright green, about 5 minutes.

Stir in the stock and salt and pepper to taste, blending well. Simmer until the vegetables are soft, about 20 minutes.

Purée the soup in a blender, food processor or pass through a fine sieve and return to the pan. Add the parsley and check the seasoning. Reheat gently until very hot. Garnish and serve. **Serves 4−6**

Savoury stuffed mushrooms

(Illustrated above and on pages 44–45)

12 large open cup mushrooms
7 g/$\frac{1}{4}$ oz (U.S. $\frac{1}{2}$ tablespoon) butter or margarine
1 onion, peeled and finely chopped
50 g/2 oz (U.S. 1 cup) wholewheat breadcrumbs
50 g/2 oz (U.S. $\frac{1}{2}$ cup) cheese, grated
1 teaspoon French mustard
$\frac{1}{2}$ teaspoon chopped fresh sage
1 egg yolk
salt and freshly ground black pepper
parsley sprigs to garnish

Trim the very tips from the mushroom stalks and discard. Finely chop the stalks.

Melt the butter or margarine in a pan. Add the chopped mushroom stalks and onion and cook over a gentle heat until softened, about 5 minutes.

Remove from the heat and add the breadcrumbs, cheese, mustard, sage, egg yolk and salt and pepper to taste, blending well.

Fill the mushroom cups with the mixture and place in a greased baking dish.

Bake in a preheated moderately hot oven (200 °C, 400 °F, Gas Mark 6) for about 15 minutes or until hot and bubbly. Serve hot, garnished with sprigs of parsley. **Serves 4**

Hot cheese bits

(Illustrated above)

1 × 100 g/4 oz slice Bucheron cheese
flour to coat
2 tablespoons fresh breadcrumbs
2 tablespoons medium oatmeal
1 egg, beaten
redcurrant purée to serve
watercress sprigs to garnish

Using a damp knife, cut the cheese into eight equal-sized pieces. Dust with flour to coat.

Mix the breadcrumbs and oatmeal on a plate. Dip the cheese cubes in the beaten egg and then coat in the oatmeal mixture. Chill until required.

Cook under a preheated hot grill (U.S. broiler) until puffed and golden, about 4 minutes, turning over once.

Serve at once with a lightly sweetened purée of redcurrants. Garnish with watercress sprigs. **Serves 2–4**

Danish Blue cheesecake

(Illustrated below)

Base
75 g/3 oz (U.S. 6 tablespoons) butter
175 g/6 oz wholewheat bran biscuits, crushed
(U.S. 2¼ cups crushed graham crackers)
Topping
100 g/4 oz Danish Blue cheese, softened
100 g/4 oz (U.S. ½ cup) cream cheese, softened
2 large eggs (sizes 1, 2), separated
1 teaspoon French mustard
garlic salt and pepper
150 ml/¼ pint double cream (U.S. ⅔ cup heavy cream)
2 teaspoons agar powder
4 tablespoons (U.S. 5 tablespoons) boiling water
To garnish
cucumber slices
black grapes

To make the base, melt the butter in a pan. Add the crushed biscuits and stir to coat. Press firmly on to the base of a 20 cm/8 inch greased loose-bottomed cake tin. Chill to set.

To make the topping, beat the cheeses until creamy. Add the egg yolks, mustard and garlic salt and pepper to taste. Stir in the cream, blending well.

Sprinkle the agar powder over the boiling water and whisk with a fork to dissolve thoroughly. Stir into the cheese mixture, blending well and leave until on the point of setting.

Whisk the egg whites until they stand in stiff peaks. Fold into the cheese mixture with a metal spoon. Pour over the biscuit base, levelling the surface. Chill until set.

Serve garnished with slices of cucumber and black grapes. Cut into wedges to serve. **Serves 6–8**

Green vegetable herb pâté

(Illustrated below)

225 g/8 oz spinach, washed
900 g/2 lb courgettes (U.S. zucchini), grated
1 tablespoon salt
50 g/2 oz (U.S. ¼ cup) butter
4 eggs
300 ml/½ pint double cream (U.S. 1¼ cups heavy cream)
3 tablespoons chive mustard
1 tablespoon chopped fresh parsley
freshly ground black pepper

Place the spinach in a pan with just the water clinging to the leaves. Cover and cook for 2 minutes, drain thoroughly. Remove and discard the stems. Use the leaves to line the base and sides of a 1.4 litre/3 pint loaf tin (U.S. 7½ cup loaf pan) lined with bakewell paper.

Meanwhile, place the courgettes in a colander, sprinkle with the salt and leave to drain for 30 minutes. Rinse and dry thoroughly.

Melt the butter in a pan. Add the courgettes and cook for 10 minutes, stirring occasionally. Leave to cool.

Beat the eggs with the cream, mustard and parsley. Add the courgettes and pepper to taste, blending well. Pour into the prepared tin, cover with foil and stand in a roasting tin containing 2.5 cm/1 inch water.

Bake in a preheated moderate oven (180°C, 350°F, Gas Mark 4) for 1¼ hours or until the pâté is firm to the touch. Allow to cool in the tin.

To serve, turn on to a serving plate, cut into slices and serve with toast. **Serves 4–6**

Meatless main meals

A meatless main meal or course is generally considered the most difficult to organize for would-be or vegetarian newcomers. The old adage of meat and two vegetables can no longer be applied and many a successful cook can crumble under the pressure of what to serve and when at a three-course meal.

There are ideas galore in this section based upon main dish staples like rice, pasta, fruit, vegetables, cereals and cheese. Cooked and served simply like Stuffed Jacket Potatoes or devised exotically and served with panache like Savoury Cheesecake, there is bound to be an idea to please.

There are cook-ahead hot dishes for hungry families to return home to; delicious one-slice-more quiches and flans for summer salad days and take-away lunch boxes; and speedy fast-food favourites when time is running short but appetites are running high. Many are low on cost and effort but high on flavour like Spiced Eggs and Cauliflower over Rice, Potato and Eggs Bombay or Savoury Cheese and Tomato Layered Loaf.

Faced with a menu to plan and still confused then turn to the ideas on pages 34–35 for inspiration – you'll see how simple it is to devise balanced meals for occasions as different as a family picnic and special occasion dinner.

For simplicity, choose a main course dish first then consider a starter and dessert to complement that decision. Remember that variety is the spice of life so vary courses for colour, flavour, texture and 'weightiness' alongside known and preferred food favourites and dislikes.

Above left: *Wholewheat pancakes (recipe page 54)*
Above right: *Savoury cheese and tomato layered loaf (recipe page 66)*
Below left: *Stuffed marrow (recipe page 65)*
Below right: *Stuffed jacket potatoes (recipe page 54)*

Wholewheat pancakes

(Illustrated on pages 52–53)

Pancake batter
100 g/4 oz (U.S. 1 cup) plain wholewheat flour
1 egg
300 ml/½ pint (U.S. 1¼ cups) milk
1 tablespoon oil
pinch of salt
Spinach and corn filling
225 g/8 oz (U.S. 1 cup) frozen leaf spinach
15 g/½ oz (U.S. 1 tablespoon) butter or margarine
1 tablespoon wholewheat flour
150 ml/¼ pint (U.S. ⅔ cup) milk
1 × 335 g/11.8 oz can sweetcorn kernels (U.S. whole
kernel corn), drained
salt and freshly ground black pepper
100 g/4 oz (U.S. 1 cup) Cheddar cheese, grated
lemon and lime slices to garnish

Place the batter ingredients in a blender and blend on maximum speed for 30 seconds.

Heat an 18 cm/7 inch omelette or crêpe pan and add a few drops of oil. Pour in 1–2 tablespoons of the batter, tilt the pan to coat the bottom evenly. Cook until the underside is brown, then turn and cook for 10 seconds. Repeat with the remaining batter, stacking the pancakes as they are cooked.

To make the filling, gently heat the spinach in a pan to thaw. Add the butter or margarine and flour, blending well. Gradually add the milk, bring to the boil, stirring constantly, and cook for 2–3 minutes. Add the sweetcorn kernels and salt and pepper to taste, blending well.

Divide the mixture evenly between the pancakes, roll up and place, seam-side down, in a shallow ovenproof dish. Cover with the grated cheese.

Bake in a preheated moderate oven (180°C, 350°F, Gas Mark 4) for 25 minutes. Garnish and serve hot. **Serves 4**

Variation
Corn and cashew filling Prepare and cook the pancakes as above. Mix 1 × 335 g/11.8 oz can sweetcorn kernels with 50 g/2 oz (U.S. ½ cup) cashew nuts, 1 tablespoon chopped fresh parsley, 1 beaten egg, 150 ml/¼ pint (U.S. ⅔ cup) natural yogurt and salt and pepper to taste, blending well. Divide the mixture evenly between the pancakes, roll up and place, seam-side down, in a shallow ovenproof dish. Cover with foil and bake in a preheated moderately hot oven (190°C, 375°F, Gas Mark 5) for 30 minutes. Serve hot.

Stuffed jacket potatoes

(Illustrated on pages 52–53)

4 × 225 g/8 oz potatoes, scrubbed
Blue cheese and cress filling
1 × 62.5 g/2½ oz packet butter with blue cheese
2 hard-boiled eggs (U.S. hard-cooked eggs), shelled
and chopped
4 teaspoons mayonnaise
1 box mustard and cress, snipped

Prick the potatoes with a fork and bake in a preheated moderately hot oven (200°C, 400°F, Gas Mark 6) for about 1 hour or until soft.

Cut a deep cross in the top of each cooked jacket potato. Gently squeeze around the base of the potato until the cross opens and the fluffy insides are exposed.

Cream the butter with blue cheese in a bowl. Stir in the chopped eggs and mayonnaise. Spoon into the hot split potatoes and sprinkle with mustard and cress. Serve at once. **Serves 4**

Variations
Crispy garlic mushroom filling Prepare and cook the potatoes as above. Heat 1 × 62.5 g/2½ oz packet butter with herbs and garlic in a pan. Add 175 g/6 oz (U.S. 1½ cups) sliced mushrooms, cover and cook for 5 minutes. Spoon the cooked mushrooms into the split potatoes.

Avocado special filling Prepare and cook the potatoes as above. Cream 1 × 62.5 g/2½ oz packet butter with lemon and parsley in a bowl. Halve, stone and mash an avocado. Mix with the butter, 1 tablespoon lemon juice and a dash of Worcestershire sauce. Spoon the avocado mixture into the split potatoes and garnish each potato with a slice of lemon.

Ploughman's filling Prepare and cook the potatoes as above. Halve each potato and scoop the flesh into a bowl. Mash with 1 × 62.5 g/2½ oz packet butter with blue cheese. Slice a few onion rings from a medium onion and reserve for garnishing. Grate the rest of the onion and stir into the potato mixture. Spoon the mixture back into the potato shells and dot equally with 1 × 62.5 g/2½ oz packet butter with blue cheese. Cook under a preheated hot grill (U.S. broiler) until golden and bubbly. Serve garnished with the onion rings and watercress sprigs.

Gnocchi with Double Gloucester and vegetables

Gnocchi with Double Gloucester and vegetables

(Illustrated below)

Gnocchi
175 g/6 oz plain flour (U.S. 1½ cups all-purpose
flour)
100 g/4 oz (U.S. ½ cup) butter
250 ml/8 fl oz (U.S. 1 cup) milk
4 eggs
100 g/4 oz Double Gloucester cheese, grated
(U.S. 1 cup grated Brick cheese)
salt and freshly ground black pepper
little French mustard (optional)
Vegetable julienne
25 g/1 oz (U.S. 2 tablespoons) butter
2 onions, peeled and sliced
4 carrots, peeled and cut into thin julienne strips
½ small head celery, scrubbed and cut into thin
julienne strips
1 recipe hot Cheese Sauce (see page 84)

To make the gnocchi, sift the flour three times. Place the butter and milk in a pan and heat gently to melt. Bring to the boil, remove from the heat, add the flour all at once and beat until smooth. Allow to cool slightly then beat in the eggs, one at a time. Fold in 75 g/3 oz (U.S. ¾ cup) of the cheese, salt and pepper to taste and a little French mustard if liked, blending well.

Shape the gnocchi using 2 dessertspoons (U.S. table-spoons) and drop into a large shallow pan of boiling water. Simmer very gently for about 10 minutes. The water should barely tremble during this time and the gnocchi will rise and float on the water.

Meanwhile melt the butter in a pan. Add the vegetable julienne and fry for 3 minutes. Spoon into a greased ovenproof gratin dish and cover with foil. Cook in a preheated moderate oven (180°C, 350°F, Gas Mark 4) for 10 minutes.

Drain the gnocchi on a dry folded teacloth. Place on top of the vegetable julienne and coat with the hot cheese sauce. Sprinkle with the remaining cheese, return to the oven and bake for a further 30 minutes. Serve hot.
Serves 4–6

Potato and eggs Bombay

(Illustrated above)

3 tablespoons (U.S. 4 tablespoons) olive oil
1 teaspoon cumin seeds
2 teaspoons mustard seeds
675 g/1½ lb potatoes, scrubbed and cut into
1 cm/½ inch cubes
1 teaspoon ground coriander
1 teaspoon garam masala
½ teaspoon turmeric
4 eggs
salt and freshly ground black pepper
1 tablespoon chopped fresh coriander
coriander sprig to garnish

Heat the oil in a medium heavy-based frying pan (U.S. skillet). Add the cumin and mustard seeds and cook for a few seconds until the seeds begin to pop.

Stir in the diced potato, coriander, garam masala and turmeric, blending well. Cover, reduce the heat and simmer gently for 15–20 minutes until the potato is just tender.

Make four hollows, evenly spaced, in the cooked potato mixture and crack an egg into each. Cover and continue cooking for a further 5 minutes or until the eggs are set.

Remove from the heat, add salt and pepper to taste and sprinkle with the coriander. Serve at once, straight from the pan. **Serves 4**

Spiced eggs and cauliflower over rice

(Illustrated above)

225 g/8 oz (U.S. generous 1 cup) long-grain rice
600 ml/1 pint (U.S. 2½ cups) water
1 teaspoon salt
2 tablespoons corn oil
1 teaspoon ground ginger
1 teaspoon ground coriander
1 teaspoon turmeric
1 small cauliflower, broken into florets
2 carrots, peeled and sliced
2 stalks celery, scrubbed and sliced
1 onion, peeled and sliced
150 ml/¼ pint (U.S. ⅔ cup) vegetable stock
150 ml/¼ pint (U.S. ⅔ cup) natural yogurt
4 hard-boiled eggs (U.S. hard-cooked eggs), halved

Place the rice, water and salt in a pan. Bring to the boil, reduce the heat, cover and simmer for 15 minutes or until the rice is tender and all the liquid has been absorbed.

Meanwhile, heat the oil in a pan. Add the ginger, coriander and turmeric and fry for 1 minute. Add the cauliflower, carrots, celery and onion and fry for 2 minutes, stirring occasionally.

Stir in the stock, blending well. Cover and simmer for 10 minutes or until the vegetables are just tender.

Add the yogurt and hard-boiled eggs. Reheat gently but do not allow to boil. Serve with rice. **Serves 4**

Rice and cheese balls

(Illustrated above)

100 g/4 oz (U.S. generous $\frac{1}{2}$ cup) long-grain rice
300 ml/$\frac{1}{2}$ pint (U.S. 1$\frac{1}{4}$ cups) water
$\frac{1}{2}$ teaspoon salt
3 tablespoons plain flour (U.S. 4 tablespoons
all-purpose flour)
2 green chillis (U.S. chilies), cored, seeded
and chopped (optional)
2 pinches bicarbonate of soda (U.S. baking
soda)
50 g/2 oz (U.S. $\frac{1}{2}$ cup) cheese, grated
$\frac{1}{2}$ teaspoon mustard powder
1 egg, beaten
about 75 g/3 oz (U.S. $\frac{3}{4}$ cup) dried breadcrumbs
oil for deep frying

Place the rice, water and salt in a pan. Bring to the boil, reduce the heat, cover and simmer for 15 minutes or until the rice is tender and all the liquid has been absorbed.

Add the flour, chillis, bicarbonate of soda, cheese and mustard, blending well.

Shape into walnut-sized balls. Dip in the beaten egg and roll in the breadcrumbs to coat.

Heat the oil in a pan to 190 °C/375 °F, or until a cube of bread browns in 1 minute, and deep fry the rice balls until cooked and golden, about 5 minutes. Drain on absorbent kitchen towel. Serve hot with a tomato sauce. **Serves 2**

Pecan and onion tart

(Illustrated above)

Pastry
225 g/8 oz (U.S. 2 cups) plain wholewheat flour
pinch of salt
100 g/4 oz (U.S. $\frac{1}{2}$ cup) butter
about 3 tablespoons water
Filling
25 g/1 oz (U.S. 2 tablespoons) butter
350 g/12 oz onions, peeled and sliced
50 g/2 oz (U.S. $\frac{1}{2}$ cup) pecan nut halves
150 ml/$\frac{1}{4}$ pint single cream (U.S. $\frac{2}{3}$ cup light cream)
2 eggs, beaten
salt and freshly ground black pepper

To make the pastry, mix the flour with the salt in a bowl. Rub in (U.S. cut in) the butter until the mixture resembles fine breadcrumbs. Add sufficient water to bind to a firm but pliable dough. Knead on a lightly floured surface until smooth and free from cracks. Roll out to a round large enough to line a 20 cm/8 inch greased flan tin.

To make the filling, melt the butter in a pan. Add the onion and fry until golden. Add the pecans, blending well. Spoon into the flan tin, spreading evenly.

Mix the cream with the eggs and salt and pepper to taste. Pour over the onion and pecan mixture.

Bake in a preheated moderately hot oven (190 °C, 375 °F, Gas Mark 5) for 40–45 minutes. Serve warm or cold garnished with parsley. **Serves 4–6**

Savoury cheesecake

(Illustrated opposite)

Base
50 g/2 oz (U.S. ¼ cup) butter
100 g/4 oz (U.S. 1½ cups) wholewheat crackers,
crushed
Topping
225 g/8 oz curd cheese (U.S. 1 cup small curd
cottage cheese)
3 eggs, separated
175 g/6 oz (U.S. 1½ cups) Mozzarella cheese, grated
150 ml/¼ pint (U.S. ⅔ cup) natural yogurt
1 teaspoon chopped fresh mixed herbs
100 g/4 oz (U.S. ⅔ cup) raisins
1 red pepper, cored, seeded and chopped
50 g/2 oz (U.S. ½ cup) mushrooms, wiped and chopped
salt and freshly ground black pepper
red pepper rings to garnish

To make the base, melt the butter in a pan. Add the cracker crumbs and mix to coat. Press into a greased 20 cm/8 inch loose-bottomed cake tin.

To make the topping, beat the curd cheese with the egg yolks. Add the Mozzarella cheese, yogurt, herbs, raisins, chopped pepper, mushrooms and salt and pepper to taste, blending well.

Whisk the egg whites until they stand in stiff peaks and fold into the cheesecake mixture with a metal spoon. Spoon over the cracker base and level the surface.

Bake in a preheated moderate oven (160°C, 325°F, Gas Mark 3) for 40–45 minutes until golden and firm to the touch. Leave to cool in the tin for 10 minutes then loosen the edges with a knife and remove from the tin. Serve warm or cold garnished with red pepper rings.
Serves 6–8

Variation
A tasty variation of the above recipe can be made by using half wholewheat crackers with half bran crackers instead of all wholewheat. Substitute the Mozzarella cheese for Gouda or Munster cheese, the raisins for sultanas (U.S. golden raisins), and the mushrooms for chopped spring onions (U.S. scallions). It isn't essential to use a red pepper, although it gives a good colour – when the seasons permit try using a green, yellow, black or white pepper, or a mixture, for added colour and flavour interest.

Lentil and raisin patties

(Illustrated opposite)

225 g/8 oz (U.S. 1 cup) red lentils
1 teaspoon curry powder
600 ml/1 pint (U.S. 2½ cups) water
1 onion, peeled and finely chopped
1 tablespoon chopped fresh parsley
1 tablespoon lemon juice
50 g/2 oz (U.S. ⅓ cup) raisins
1 tablespoon tomato purée
salt and freshly ground black pepper
1 egg, beaten
75 g/3 oz (U.S. 1½ cups) wholewheat breadcrumbs
oil for shallow frying
To garnish
cucumber slices
sliced radishes
parsley sprigs

Rinse the lentils and place in a pan with the curry powder and water. Bring to the boil, reduce the heat and simmer, partially covered, for about 20 minutes until tender.

Add the onion, parsley, lemon juice, raisins, tomato purée and salt and pepper to taste, blending well. Cook gently for about 5 minutes, stirring occasionally, until thick. Allow to cool.

Divide and shape into eight patties. Dip in the beaten egg and coat in the breadcrumbs.

Heat about 5 mm/¼ inch oil in a frying pan (U.S. skillet) and fry the patties for about 8 minutes, turning once, until golden. Drain on absorbent kitchen towel.

Garnish with cucumber slices, sliced radishes and parsley sprigs. Serve piping hot with jacket baked potatoes and a green vegetable or salad. **Serves 4**

Above: Savoury cheesecake
Below: Lentil and raisin patties

Parsnip and corn layer

(Illustrated below)

1 tablespoon oil
675 g/1½ lb parsnips, peeled and cut into
1 cm/½ inch cubes
450 g/1 lb tomatoes, skinned and sliced
1 × 335 g/11.8 oz can sweetcorn kernels (U.S. whole
kernel corn), drained
175 g/6 oz (U.S. 1½ cups) Cheddar cheese, grated
150 ml/¼ pint (U.S. ⅔ cup) natural yogurt
salt and freshly ground black pepper
50 g/2 oz (U.S. 1 cup) wholewheat breadcrumbs

Heat the oil in a pan. Add the parsnips and sauté until softened, about 5 minutes.

Place a layer of parsnips in the base of a medium-sized ovenproof dish. Top with a layer of tomatoes and sweetcorn.

Mix half of the cheese with the yogurt and salt and pepper to taste. Pour over the vegetables. Repeat the parsnip, tomato and sweetcorn layers once more.

Mix the remaining cheese with the breadcrumbs and sprinkle over the top of the vegetables.

Bake in a preheated moderate oven (180°C, 350°F, Gas Mark 4) for 30 minutes. Serve hot, straight from the dish. **Serves 4**

Variations

Potato and corn layer Prepare as above but use 675 g/1½ lb potatoes, peeled and cut into 1 cm/½ inch cubes instead of the parsnips. Sauté in the oil for about 8 minutes until softened.

Peppered parsnip and corn layer Prepare and cook as above but use 1 × 326 g/11½ oz can sweetcorn kernels with mixed peppers (U.S. whole kernel corn with mixed peppers) instead of plain sweetcorn. Toss the breadcrumbs with a dash of chilli powder if liked for a spicy-topped savoury main course dish.

Herbed parsnip and corn layer Prepare and cook as above but use a cheese made with chopped herbs or flavour the natural yogurt with 1–2 teaspoons chopped fresh herbs.

Vegetarian lasagne

(Illustrated below)

1 tablespoon oil
2 onions, peeled and chopped
2 red peppers, cored, seeded and sliced
2 green peppers, cored, seeded and sliced
1 × 425 g/15 oz can peeled tomatoes
1 garlic clove, peeled and crushed
175 g/6 oz (U.S. $\frac{3}{4}$ cup) tomato purée
1 teaspoon fresh mixed herbs
salt and freshly ground black pepper
175 g/6 oz plain or wholewheat lasagne
1 recipe Cheese Sauce (see page 84)
25 g/1 oz (U.S. $\frac{1}{4}$ cup) Cheddar cheese, grated

Heat the oil in a pan. Add the onions and peppers and cook over a gentle heat until softened, about 5 minutes. Stir in the tomatoes, garlic, tomato purée, herbs and salt and pepper to taste, blending well. Simmer over a gentle heat until thickened and reduced, about 30 minutes.

Meanwhile, boil the lasagne until tender or 'al dente' according to the packet instructions. Drain thoroughly.

Line a greased shallow ovenproof dish with lasagne. Cover with a little of the tomato mixture. Top with another layer of pasta. Continue layering in this way until all the pasta and sauce have been used, finishing with a layer of lasagne.

Cover with the cheese sauce and sprinkle with the grated cheese. Bake in a preheated moderate oven (180°C, 350°F, Gas Mark 4) for 45 minutes. Serve hot with a mixed salad. **Serves 6**

Variation
Vegetarian lasagne with nuts Prepare and cook as above but add 25 g/1 oz (U.S. $\frac{1}{4}$ cup) chopped nuts to the cheese sauce prior to baking. About 10 minutes before the end of the cooking time, sprinkle the lasagne with a further 15 g/$\frac{1}{2}$ oz (U.S. 1–2 tablespoons) chopped nuts to give a crunchy golden topping.

Vegetable curry

(Illustrated above)

2 tablespoons oil
1 onion, peeled and chopped
1 tablespoon curry powder
1 teaspoon paprika
2 teaspoons tomato purée
1 teaspoon lemon juice
1 tablespoon apricot jam or redcurrant jelly
300 ml/½ pint (U.S. 1¼ cups) milk
50 g/2 oz raisins or sultanas (U.S. ⅓ cup raisins or golden raisins)
900 g/2 lb mixed prepared vegetables (e.g. sliced carrots, cauliflower florets and diced potato)
4 hard-boiled eggs (U.S. 4 hard-cooked eggs), shelled and sliced or halved

Place the oil in a pan. Add the onion and fry gently for 5 minutes. Stir in the curry powder and paprika, blending well. Cook for a further 3 minutes.

Add the tomato purée, lemon juice, jam or jelly, milk and raisins or sultanas, blending well. Bring to the boil, reduce the heat and simmer, uncovered, for 10 minutes.

Meanwhile, cook the vegetables in a pan of boiling salted water for 10 minutes. Drain thoroughly and add to the curry sauce. Cook over a gentle heat until the vegetables are tender, about 10–15 minutes.

Add the hard-boiled eggs, mixing well. Spoon into a warmed dish and garnish with watercress. Serve with a chutney and cucumber with yogurt. **Serves 4**

Cheese and noodle hot pot

(Illustrated above)

225 g/8 oz ribbon noodles
50 g/2 oz (U.S. ¼ cup) butter
1 onion, peeled and chopped
25 g/1 oz (U.S. ¼ cup) flour
300 ml/½ pint (U.S. 1¼ cups) milk
2 tablespoons tomato purée
50 g/2 oz (U.S. ½ cup) hazelnuts, roughly chopped
225 g/8 oz (U.S. 1 cup) cottage cheese
salt and freshly ground black pepper
50 g/2 oz (U.S. ½ cup) cheese, grated
To garnish
1 tomato, sliced
parsley sprigs

Cook the noodles in a pan of boiling salted water until tender, according to the packet instructions. Drain.

Meanwhile, melt half the butter in a pan. Add the onion and fry until golden, about 10 minutes.

Place the remaining butter, flour and milk in a pan and heat, whisking constantly, until the sauce thickens. Stir in the noodles, onion, tomato purée, hazelnuts, cottage cheese and salt and pepper to taste, blending well. Spoon into a 1.2 litre/2 pint (U.S. 2½ pint) greased ovenproof dish and sprinkle with the grated cheese.

Cook in a preheated moderately hot oven (190°C, 375°F, Gas Mark 5) until golden. Serve hot. **Serves 4**

Mid-week lentil and corn pie

(Illustrated above)

225 g/8 oz (U.S. 1 cup) red lentils
1 tablespoon oil
1 onion, peeled and chopped
2 carrots, peeled and roughly chopped
1 green pepper, cored, seeded and chopped
1 × 398 g/14 oz can peeled tomatoes, coarsely chopped
1 × 335 g/11.8 oz can sweetcorn kernels (U.S. whole kernel corn), drained
salt and freshly ground black pepper
450 g/1 lb potatoes, peeled, boiled and mashed
2 tablespoons milk

Rinse and place the lentils in a pan. Cover with cold water, bring to the boil, reduce the heat and simmer until tender, about 20–30 minutes. Drain thoroughly.

Meanwhile, heat the oil in a pan. Add the onion, carrot and green pepper and fry gently for 10 minutes.

Add the tomatoes and sweetcorn kernels, blending well. Simmer gently for 15 minutes. Add the lentils and salt and pepper to taste, blending well. Place in an ovenproof dish.

Mix the potatoes with the milk, then spoon or pipe attractively on top of the lentil mixture. Cook under a preheated hot grill (U.S. broiler) until golden. Serve hot. **Serves 4**

Savoury Bramley pasties

(Illustrated above)

100 g/4 oz (U.S. ⅔ cup) potato, peeled and coarsely grated
175 g/6 oz Bramley apples, peeled, cored and chopped (U.S. 1½ cups chopped baking or tart apples)
2 tablespoons finely chopped onion
175 g/6 oz (U.S. 1½ cups) Cheddar cheese, grated
2 hard-boiled eggs (U.S. 2 hard-cooked eggs), chopped
1 teaspoon Worcestershire sauce
½ teaspoon dried thyme
2 tablespoons soured cream or natural yogurt
salt and freshly ground black pepper
1 recipe Wholewheat Pastry (see page 57)
beaten egg to glaze

Mix the potato with the apple, onion, cheese, eggs, Worcestershire sauce, thyme, soured cream or yogurt and salt and pepper to taste, blending well.

Cut the prepared pastry into five equal pieces. Roll out each thinly to an 18 cm/7 inch round.

Divide the filling between the pastry rounds, lightly dampen the edges with water and draw up to meet in the centre to make pasties. Crimp the edges and place on a greased baking tray. Glaze with beaten egg.

Bake in a preheated moderately hot oven (200 °C, 400 °F, Gas Mark 6) for about 25 minutes or until lightly browned. Serve hot, warm or cold. **Makes 5**

Vegetable casserole

(Illustrated opposite and on the cover)

25 g/1 oz (U.S. 2 tablespoons) butter
2 onions, peeled and sliced
2 garlic cloves, peeled and crushed
225 g/8 oz (U.S. 1 cup) carrots, peeled and sliced
4 stalks celery, scrubbed and sliced
1 potato, peeled and diced
2 tablespoons paprika
100 g/4 oz (U.S. $\frac{2}{3}$ cup) cooked red kidney beans
300 ml/$\frac{1}{2}$ pint (U.S. 1$\frac{1}{4}$ cups) vegetable stock
450 ml/$\frac{3}{4}$ pint (U.S. 2 cups) milk
2 tablespoons tomato purée
2 tablespoons cornflour (U.S. cornstarch)

Melt the butter in a large pan. Add the onions, garlic, carrots, celery, potato and paprika and fry over a moderate heat for 5 minutes.

Add the kidney beans, stock, almost all of the milk and the tomato purée, blending well. Bring to the boil, reduce the heat, cover and simmer for 30 minutes.

Blend the cornflour with the remaining milk. Stir into the casserole and cook, stirring constantly, until thickened. Serve hot with jacket baked potatoes.
Serves 4

Variations
Black-eye bean and vegetable casserole Prepare as above but use 100 g/4 oz (U.S. $\frac{2}{3}$ cup) cooked black-eye beans instead of the red kidney beans. Add to the vegetable mixture, bring to the boil, reduce the heat and simmer, covered, for 20–25 minutes.
Chilli vegetable casserole Prepare and cook as above but add 1–2 teaspoons (according to taste) chilli powder to the onion mixture. Serve hot with crispy corn chips instead of jacket baked potatoes if liked.

Stuffed marrow

(Illustrated on pages 52–53)

175 g/6 oz (U.S. $\frac{3}{4}$ cup) continental lentils, soaked in cold water for 3 hours
2 tablespoons oil
1 large onion, peeled and sliced
1 garlic clove, peeled and crushed
2 stalks celery, scrubbed and chopped
1 × 335 g/11.8 oz can sweetcorn kernels with peppers (U.S. whole kernel corn with peppers), drained
50 g/2 oz (U.S. $\frac{1}{3}$ cup) brown rice, cooked
1 teaspoon ground coriander
2 tablespoons chopped fresh parsley
150 ml/$\frac{1}{4}$ pint (U.S. $\frac{2}{3}$ cup) natural yogurt
1 egg, beaten
50 g/2 oz (U.S. $\frac{1}{2}$ cup) Cheshire cheese, crumbled
1 medium-sized marrow (U.S. summer squash)

Place the lentils in a pan with cold water to cover. Bring to the boil, reduce the heat and simmer for about 45 minutes or until tender. Drain thoroughly.

Heat the oil in a pan. Add the onion and garlic and fry for 5 minutes. Add the celery and sweetcorn kernels with peppers, blending well. Cook for a further 5 minutes. Add the lentils, rice, coriander, parsley, yogurt, egg and cheese, blending well.

Cut the marrow into four thick rings. Peel, if preferred, and remove the seeds from the centre with a spoon. Blanch in a pan of boiling water for 4 minutes. Drain and place in a shallow ovenproof dish.

Fill the hollows of the marrow with the stuffing. Cover with foil. Bake in a preheated moderate oven (180°C, 350°F, Gas Mark 4) for about 35 minutes or until the marrow is tender. Serve hot with baked tomatoes. **Serves 4**

Variation
Stuffed courgettes Prepare and cook as above but use 4 large courgettes (U.S. zucchini) instead of the marrow. Halve each courgette lengthways, scoop out the seeds, blanch as above and fill with the stuffing. Do not peel the courgettes unless the skin is very tough and serve 2 stuffed courgette halves per portion.

Vegetable casserole

Vegetable cobbler

(Illustrated opposite)

25 g/1 oz (U.S. 2 tablespoons) butter
1 onion, peeled and chopped
2 carrots, peeled and chopped
1 courgette (U.S. zucchini), trimmed and sliced
2 stalks celery, scrubbed and chopped
100 g/4 oz (U.S. 1 cup) mushrooms, wiped and sliced
3 tomatoes, skinned and quartered
1 × 425 g/15 oz can cassoulet beans
salt and freshly ground black pepper
Topping
75 g/3 oz (U.S. ¾ cup) plain wholewheat flour
75 g/3 oz plain flour (U.S. ¾ cup all-purpose flour)
1 teaspoon baking powder
½ teaspoon mustard powder
25 g/1 oz (U.S. 2 tablespoons) butter
75 g/3 oz (U.S. ¾ cup) Cheddar cheese, grated
1 egg, beaten
2–3 tablespoons milk

Melt the butter in a large pan. Add the onion and cook for 3 minutes. Add the carrots and cook for a further 2–3 minutes. Stir in the courgette, celery and mushrooms, blending well. Cover and cook for 5 minutes, stirring occasionally. Stir in the tomatoes, beans and salt and pepper to taste.

Meanwhile, to make the topping, mix the flours with the baking powder, a pinch of salt and the mustard powder. Rub in (U.S. cut in) the butter until the mixture resembles fine breadcrumbs. Stir in 50 g/2 oz (U.S. ½ cup) of the cheese. Bind together with the egg and sufficient milk to make a soft dough.

Roll out the dough on a lightly floured surface to about 2 cm/¾ inch thick. Stamp out about 10–12 rounds using a 6 cm/2¼ inch cutter.

Spoon the vegetable mixture into an ovenproof dish and top with the rounds, arranged overlapping around the edge of the dish. Brush with a little milk and sprinkle with the remaining cheese.

Bake in a preheated hot oven (220°C, 425°F, Gas Mark 7) for 20 minutes. Serve hot. **Serves 4**

Savoury cheese and tomato layered loaf

(Illustrated on pages 52–53)

6 small field mushrooms, peeled
25 g/1 oz (U.S. 2 tablespoons) savoury butter with black pepper
175 g/6 oz (U.S. 3 cups) fresh breadcrumbs
100 g/4 oz mature Cheddar cheese (U.S. 1 cup sharp Cheddar cheese), grated
½ green pepper, cored, seeded and chopped
1 onion, peeled and finely chopped
50 g/2 oz (U.S. ½ cup) walnuts, chopped
1 teaspoon mustard powder
1 teaspoon salt
2 eggs, beaten
3 tomatoes, skinned and sliced
4 tablespoons (U.S. 5 tablespoons) tomato ketchup
To garnish
tomato wedges
watercress sprigs

Cut the stalks off the mushrooms and arrange the caps, stalk side down, in the base of a greased 1 kg/2 lb loaf tin. Dot the mushrooms with half of the savoury butter.

Mix the breadcrumbs with the cheese, chopped pepper, onion, walnuts, mustard and salt. Stir in the eggs, blending well.

Spoon half of the breadcrumb mixture on top of the mushrooms and press down with the back of a spoon. Arrange the tomato slices on top and dot with the remaining savoury butter.

Stir the tomato ketchup into the remaining breadcrumb mixture, blending well. Spoon on top of the tomatoes and press down firmly.

Bake in a preheated moderately hot oven (200°C, 400°F, Gas Mark 6) for 45 minutes. Turn out of the tin on to a warmed serving plate. Garnish and serve hot with green vegetables or cold with salad. **Serves 4–6**

Vegetable cobbler

Vegetable bake

(Illustrated above)

75 g/3 oz (U.S. 6 tablespoons) butter
2 small onions, peeled and sliced
225 g/8 oz courgettes, trimmed and sliced
(U.S. 1¾ cups sliced zucchini)
225 g/8 oz (U.S. 1 cup) tomatoes, sliced
1 teaspoon dried mixed herbs
salt and freshly ground black pepper
50 g/2 oz (U.S. ½ cup) flour
600 ml/1 pint (U.S. 2½ cups) milk
175 g/6 oz (U.S. 1½ cups) Danish Cheddar cheese, grated
50 g/2 oz (U.S. 1 cup) fresh breadcrumbs
To garnish
tomato wedges
parsley sprig

Melt 25 g/1 oz (U.S. 2 tablespoons) of the butter in a pan. Add the onions and fry until soft, about 10 minutes.

Place half of the courgettes in an ovenproof dish and cover with half of the cooked onions and all of the tomatoes. Sprinkle with the herbs and salt and pepper to taste. Add the remaining onions and courgettes.

Place the remaining butter, flour and milk in a pan. Heat, whisking constantly, until the sauce thickens. Remove from the heat and stir in 100 g/4 oz (U.S. 1 cup) of the cheese, blending well. Pour over the vegetable mixture, sprinkle with the breadcrumbs and remaining cheese.

Bake in a preheated moderate oven (180°C, 350°F, Gas Mark 4) for 30 minutes. Serve hot, garnished with tomato wedges and a parsley sprig. Accompany with crusty bread and butter. **Serves 4**

Blue cheese parcels

(Illustrated above)

225 g/8 oz (u.s. 2 cups) wholewheat flour
100 g/4 oz plain flour (u.s. 1 cup all-purpose flour)
100 g/4 oz (u.s. ½ cup) butter
150 g/5 oz (u.s. 1¼ cups) Danish Blue cheese, grated
about 5 tablespoons cold water
175 g/6 oz (u.s. 1½ cups) carrots, peeled and
coarsely grated
225 g/8 oz (u.s. 1⅓ cups) potatoes, peeled and diced
175 g/6 oz (u.s. 1½ cups) onions, peeled and chopped
1½ teaspoons dried mixed herbs
3 tablespoons (u.s. 4 tablespoons) vegetable stock
salt and freshly ground black pepper

Mix the flours in a bowl. Rub in (u.s. cut in) the butter until the mixture resembles fine breadcrumbs. Stir in 100 g/4 oz (u.s. 1 cup) of the cheese and sufficient water to bind to a soft but not sticky dough. Knead on a lightly floured surface until smooth and free from cracks.

Divide the dough into four equal pieces. Roll out each piece to an 18 cm/7 inch round.

Mix the carrot with the potato, onion, remaining cheese, herbs, stock and salt and pepper to taste, blending well. Divide between the pastry rounds, lightly dampen the edges with water and draw up to meet in the centre to make parcels. Crimp the edges and place on a greased baking tray.

Bake in a preheated moderately hot oven (200 °C, 400 °F, Gas Mark 6) for 20 minutes. Reduce the oven temperature to moderate (180 °C, 350 °F, Gas Mark 4) and bake for a further 15–20 minutes. Serve hot or cold with vegetable crudités, if liked. **Makes 4**

69

Spinach and Brie flan

(Illustrated opposite)

Pastry
75 g/3 oz plain flour (U.S. ¾ cup all-purpose flour)
75 g/3 oz (U.S. ¾ cup) wholewheat flour
pinch of salt
75 g/3 oz (U.S. 6 tablespoons) butter or margarine
3–4 tablespoons cold water
Filling
275 g/10 oz Brie
100 g/4 oz spinach leaves, washed and finely shredded
2 eggs
150 ml/¼ pint (U.S. ⅔ cup) milk
salt and freshly ground black pepper
3 tablespoons double cream (U.S. 4 tablespoons
heavy cream)
pinch of grated nutmeg

To make the pastry, place the flours and salt in a bowl. Rub in (U.S. cut in) the butter or margarine until the mixture resembles fine breadcrumbs. Add the water and mix to a firm but pliable dough.

Roll out the pastry on a lightly floured surface to a round large enough to line a greased 20 cm/8 inch flan ring set on a baking tray. Chill while preparing the filling.

To make the filling, trim the rind from the cheese and cut the cheese into cubes. Place the shredded spinach on the pastry base and tuck in the pieces of Brie.

Beat the eggs with the milk and salt and pepper to taste. Pour over the flan evenly. Spoon the cream over the surface and sprinkle with nutmeg.

Bake in a preheated moderately hot oven (190°C, 375°F, Gas Mark 5) for 35–40 minutes. Serve warm or cold, cut into wedges. **Serves 4**

Curried cheese tart

(Illustrated opposite)

Pastry
75 g/3 oz plain flour (U.S. ¾ cup all-purpose flour)
75 g/3 oz (U.S. ¾ cup) wholewheat flour
pinch of salt
75 g/3 oz (U.S. 6 tablespoons) butter or margarine
3–4 tablespoons cold water
Filling
1 tablespoon oil
1 red pepper, cored, seeded and sliced
2 tablespoons mango chutney
150 g/5 oz (U.S. 1¼ cups) Red Leicester cheese, grated
50 g/2 oz (U.S. ½ cup) walnuts, chopped
½–1 teaspoon curry powder
2 eggs, beaten
150 ml/¼ pint single cream (U.S. ⅔ cup light cream)
2 tablespoons chopped fresh parsley
salt and freshly ground black pepper

To make the pastry, place the flours and salt in a bowl. Rub in (U.S. cut in) the butter or margarine until the mixture resembles fine breadcrumbs. Add the water and mix to a firm but pliable dough.

Roll out the pastry on a lightly floured surface and use to line as 18 cm/7 inch square flan dish or shallow cake tin. Chill while preparing the filling.

To make the filling, heat the oil in a small pan. Add the pepper and cook until softened, about 5 minutes. Spread the mango chutney over the pastry base and sprinkle with the cooked pepper.

Mix the cheese with the walnuts, curry powder, eggs, cream, parsley and salt and pepper to taste, blending well. Pour into the pastry case.

Bake in a preheated moderate oven (180°C, 350°F, Gas Mark 4) for 35–40 minutes. Serve warm or cold. **Serves 6**

Variation
Spanish cheese tart Prepare and cook as above but fill the tart with a mixture of 1 chopped red and green pepper, 1 small chopped onion, 50 g/2 oz (U.S. ½ cup) chopped mushrooms, 2 chopped courgettes (U.S. zucchini) and 6 sliced green olives sautéed in 25 g/1 oz (U.S. 2 table-spoons) butter. Mix with 2 beaten eggs, 150 ml/¼ pint double cream (U.S. ⅔ cup heavy cream), 50 g/2 oz (U.S. ½ cup) grated cheese and salt and pepper to taste. This tart is best served warm, cut into wedges, with a crisp seasonal side salad tossed in an oil and vinegar dressing.

Above: *Spinach and Brie flan*
Below: *Curried cheese tart*

Light lunches, appetizers and snacks

A light lunch for two to break the day; a tray full of nibbles to serve with pre-dinner drinks; or a speedy yet sustaining snack to replace or 'stretch' a meal time – all are requirements met in this recipe section.

There are ideas for fresh winter and summer salads, light but nourishing soups, simple tossed pasta, creamy and delicate egg dishes, bubbling pizzas and sizzling stir-frys.

The majority assume that for such meals time is at a premium and so can be prepared at a moment's notice, or at the very least can be made ahead then quickly cooked to perfection when required. Without doubt, most can also be used as part of a cold or hot table buffet when several dishes are presented.

Such light meal dishes can also be 'stretched' to cope with late-comers or larger-than-anticipated appetites with slices of wholewheat bread, crackers, wedges of cheese, a freshly-laden bowl of fruit, nuts or seeds. Then dip into the freezer for an 'instant' light dessert like frozen Banana and Honey Ice-cream to crown the meal.

Snacks can be even more impromptu – but remember if you're a one-main-meal-a-day-plus-snacks person to have a well-stocked store-cupboard, refrigerator and freezer of easily assembled ingredients like crispbreads, dried fruit, nuts, eggs, a good selection of cheeses and many fresh as well as canned bread and savoury cracker toppings.

Above: *Corn and rye snack (recipe page 74)*
Below left: *Tuscany pizza (recipe page 79)*
Right: *Vegetable and pasta stir-fry (recipe page 79)*

Italian lunchtime pasties

(Illustrated opposite)

Pastry
350 g/12 oz plain flour (U.S. 3 cups all-purpose flour)
pinch of salt
175 g/6 oz (U.S. ¾ cup) butter or margarine
about 5 tablespoons cold water
Filling
25 g/1 oz (U.S. 2 tablespoons) butter
1 large onion, peeled and sliced
100 g/4 oz (U.S. 1 cup) mushrooms, wiped and sliced
50 g/2 oz (U.S. ½ cup) green cabbage, shredded
1 × 450 g/1 lb can baked beans in tomato sauce
1 teaspoon dried oregano
salt and freshly ground black pepper

Mix the flour and salt in a bowl. Rub in (U.S. cut in) the butter until the mixture resembles fine breadcrumbs. Stir in sufficient water to bind to a soft but not sticky dough. Knead on a lightly floured surface until smooth and free from cracks.

Meanwhile, melt the butter in a pan. Add the onion and cook gently for about 5 minutes. Add the mushrooms and cabbage and cook for a further 5 minutes, stirring occasionally.

Add the beans, oregano and salt and pepper to taste, blending well. Leave until cold.

Cut the dough into four equal pieces and roll out each on a lightly floured surface to an 18 cm/7 inch round.

Divide the bean mixture between the pastry rounds, lightly dampen the pastry edges with water and draw up to meet in the centre to make pasties. Crimp the edges and place on a greased baking tray.

Bake in a preheated moderately hot oven (200°C, 400°F, Gas Mark 6) for 20 minutes. Reduce the oven temperature to moderate (180°C, 350°F, Gas Mark 4) and bake for a further 15–20 minutes. Serve warm or cold. **Makes 4**

Corn and rye snack

(Illustrated on pages 72–73)

225 g/8 oz (U.S. 1 cup) cottage cheese
6 spring onions (U.S. scallions), trimmed and chopped
1 × 335 g/11.8 oz can sweetcorn kernels (U.S. whole kernel corn), drained
salt and freshly ground black pepper
rye crispbreads
2 hard-boiled eggs (U.S. hard-cooked eggs), shelled and sliced
To garnish
small parsley sprigs
spring onion (U.S. scallion) tassels (optional)
lime slices (optional)

Mix the cottage cheese with the spring onions, sweetcorn kernels and salt and pepper to taste, blending well.

Spoon generously on to rye crispbreads. Lay slices of hard-boiled egg on top and garnish with small sprigs of parsley, spring onion tassels and lime slices. Serve at once. **Serves 4–6**

Variations
Egg and rye snack Mix 2 tablespoons shredded white cabbage with 1 tablespoon grated carrot, 2 chopped spring onions (U.S. scallions), 2 chopped hard-boiled eggs (U.S. hard-cooked eggs), 2 tablespoons mayonnaise and salt and pepper to taste. Spoon generously on to rye crispbreads and top with slices of hard-boiled egg (from 2 eggs). Garnish with sprigs of watercress.
Leek and rye snack Mix 1 large finely sliced leek with 1 teaspoon grated lemon rind, 2 tablespoons raisins, 2 tablespoons mayonnaise and salt and pepper to taste. Spoon generously on to rye crispbreads and garnish with slices of hard-boiled egg (from 2 eggs). Sprinkle with a few chopped herbs, chopped capers, toasted sesame seeds or sprigs of watercress, parsley or coriander if liked.

Italian lunchtime pasties

Herb dressed cheese salad

(Illustrated above)

225 g/8 oz Saint Paulin cheese
5 tablespoons (u.s. 6 tablespoons) grapeseed oil
2 tablespoons lemon juice
2 teaspoons chopped fresh parsley
8 leaves fresh basil, finely chopped
salt and freshly ground black pepper
4 large ripe firm tomatoes, skinned and sliced
8 spring onions (u.s. scallions), trimmed and chopped
To garnish
lemon slices
black olives (u.s. ripe olives)

Rind and slice the cheese finely with a serrated knife and place in a shallow dish.

Beat the oil with the lemon juice, parsley, basil and salt and pepper to taste. Pour over the cheese slices, cover and leave to marinate for 30 minutes.

To serve, arrange the tomato slices equally on four individual serving plates. Top with the cheese and a little spring onion. Garnish with lemon slices and olives.

Serve with warm crusty bread to mop up the herby lemon juices. **Serves 4**

Crusty mushroom loaf

(Illustrated above)

1 small wholewheat crusty loaf
50 g/2 oz (u.s. $\frac{1}{4}$ cup) butter
50 g/2 oz (u.s. $\frac{1}{2}$ cup) flour
600 ml/1 pint (u.s. $2\frac{1}{2}$ cups) milk
225 g/8 oz (u.s. 2 cups) open cup mushrooms, wiped and sliced
2 tablespoons chopped fresh parsley
2 hard-boiled eggs (u.s. hard-cooked eggs), shelled and chopped
salt and freshly ground black pepper

Cut a 1 cm/$\frac{1}{2}$ inch slice lengthways off the top of the loaf and carefully pull out the soft bread inside (use to make breadcrumbs for another dish). Replace the lid and place on a baking tray. Cook in a preheated moderate oven (180°C, 350°F, Gas Mark 4) for about 15 minutes until crisp.

Meanwhile, to make the filling, melt the butter in a pan. Stir in the flour and cook for 1 minute. Remove from the heat and gradually add the milk, blending well. Bring to the boil and cook for 2–3 minutes, stirring constantly, until smooth and thickened.

Stir in the mushrooms, parsley, egg and salt and pepper to taste, blending well.

Fill the bread loaf shell with the mushroom mixture and replace the lid. Return to the oven and bake for 10 minutes. Serve hot, cut into thick slices with a seasonal salad garnish. **Serves 4**

Apple and potato soup pot

(Illustrated above)

3 tablespoons (U.S. 4 tablespoons) oil
350 g/12 oz onions, peeled and sliced
450 g/1 lb Bramley apples, peeled, cored and sliced
(U.S. 4 cups sliced baking or tart apples)
900 g/2 lb potatoes, peeled and sliced
300 ml/½ pint cider (U.S. 1¼ cups hard cider)
1.2 litres/2 pints (U.S. 5 cups) well-flavoured
vegetable stock
½ teaspoon dried mixed herbs
½ teaspoon ground coriander
salt and freshly ground black pepper
100 ml/4 fl oz single cream (U.S. ½ cup light cream)
chopped fresh mint or snipped chives to garnish

Heat the oil in a large pan. Add the onions and cook until softened, about 5–8 minutes. Add the apples and potatoes and cook for a further 10 minutes, stirring frequently.

Stir in the cider and cook briskly for 10 minutes. Add the stock, herbs, coriander and salt and pepper to taste, blending well. Cover and simmer for 40–60 minutes.

Purée the soup in a blender, food processor or pass through a fine sieve and return to the pan. Stir in the cream and check the seasoning. Reheat gently but do not boil. Serve hot, sprinkled with chopped mint or snipped chives. **Serves 4–6**

Two-cheese spaghetti

(Illustrated above)

450 g/1 lb wholewheat or plain spaghetti
65 g/2½ oz (U.S. 5 tablespoons) butter
100 g/4 oz (U.S. 1 cup) button mushrooms, sliced
40 g/1½ oz (U.S. 6 tablespoons) flour
600 ml/1 pint (U.S. 2½ cups) milk
100 g/4 oz (U.S. 1 cup) Edam cheese, grated
salt and freshly ground black pepper
75 g/3 oz (U.S. ¾ cup) Cheddar cheese, grated

Cook the spaghetti in a pan of boiling salted water until tender or 'al dente' according to the packet instructions.

Meanwhile, melt 25 g/1 oz (U.S. 2 tablespoons) of the butter in a pan. Add the mushrooms and sauté until just tender, about 5 minutes. Remove from the pan with a slotted spoon and set aside.

Add the remaining butter to the pan juices and heat to melt. Stir in the flour and cook for 1 minute. Remove from the heat and gradually add the milk, blending well. Bring to the boil and cook for 2–3 minutes, stirring constantly, until smooth and thickened.

Add the Edam cheese and salt and pepper to taste to the sauce, blending well.

Drain the spaghetti, return to the pan and add the mushrooms and cheese sauce. Toss gently to mix then spoon into a flameproof dish.

Sprinkle with the Cheddar cheese and cook under a preheated hot grill (U.S. broiler) until golden. Serve at once. **Serves 4**

Vegetable and pasta stir-fry

(Illustrated opposite and on pages 72–73)

450 g/1 lb wholewheat pasta shells
75 g/3 oz (U.S. 6 tablespoons) butter
1 large onion, peeled and sliced
3 stalks celery, scrubbed and cut into strips
2 large carrots, peeled and cut into strips
75 g/3 oz (U.S. $\frac{3}{4}$ cup) French beans, topped and tailed
1 small red pepper, cored, seeded and sliced
1 small green or yellow pepper, cored, seeded and sliced
2 tablespoons soy sauce
salt and freshly ground black pepper
75 g/3 oz (U.S. $\frac{3}{4}$ cup) cheese, grated (optional)

Cook the pasta in a pan of boiling salted water until tender or 'al dente' according to the packet instructions. Drain and refresh under cold water.

Melt the butter in a large frying pan (U.S. skillet) or wok. Add the onion, celery, carrots, beans and peppers. Stir-fry over a gentle heat for about 10 minutes until softened.

Add the cooked pasta, soy sauce and salt and pepper to taste, blending well. Cook for a further 2 minutes to reheat the pasta. Serve at once, sprinkled with cheese if liked. **Serves 4**

Vegetable pilaff

(Illustrated opposite)

50 g/2 oz (U.S. $\frac{1}{4}$ cup) butter
1 onion, peeled and sliced
1 garlic clove, peeled and crushed
2 stalks celery, scrubbed and sliced
225 g/8 oz (U.S. generous 1 cup) brown rice
100 g/4 oz (U.S. 1 cup) button mushrooms, wiped and sliced
1 × 335 g/11.8 oz can sweetcorn kernels with peppers (U.S. whole kernel corn with peppers), drained
600 ml/1 pint (U.S. $2\frac{1}{2}$ cups) vegetable stock
50 g/2 oz (U.S. $\frac{1}{3}$ cup) raisins
50 g/2 oz (U.S. $\frac{1}{2}$ cup) chopped nuts

Melt the butter in a pan. Add the onion, garlic and celery and cook until softened, about 5 minutes. Add the rice, blending well and cook for a further 5 minutes, stirring occasionally.

Stir in the mushrooms, sweetcorn kernels with peppers and stock. Bring to the boil then transfer to a casserole.

Cover and cook in a preheated moderate oven (180 °C, 350 °F, Gas Mark 4) for 35 minutes.

Stir in the raisins and nuts, blending well. Add a little extra stock if necessary, then cover and cook for a further 10 minutes. Serve hot. **Serves 4**

Tuscany pizza

(Illustrated on pages 72–73)

Base
225 g/8 oz (U.S. 2 cups) wholewheat flour
1 teaspoon salt
1 teaspoon easy blend dried yeast
25 g/1 oz (U.S. 2 tablespoons) butter or margarine
150 ml/$\frac{1}{4}$ pint (U.S. $\frac{2}{3}$ cup) warm milk
1 egg, beaten
Topping
2 tablespoons olive oil
175 g/6 oz aubergine, cut into 1 cm/$\frac{1}{2}$ inch cubes (U.S. $1\frac{1}{2}$ cups cubed eggplant)
1 green pepper, cored, seeded and sliced
1 small onion, peeled and sliced
1 garlic clove, peeled and crushed
1 × 335 g/11.8 oz can sweetcorn kernels (U.S. whole kernel corn), drained
1 × 398 g/14 oz can peeled tomatoes, drained
salt and freshly ground black pepper
100 g/4 oz (U.S. $\frac{1}{4}$ lb) Mozzarella cheese, sliced
few black olives (U.S. ripe olives)

To make the base, mix the flour with the salt and yeast in a bowl. Rub in (U.S. cut in) the butter or margarine until the mixture resembles fine breadcrumbs. Stir in the milk and egg and mix to a soft dough. Turn on to a lightly floured surface and knead until smooth and elastic. Return to the bowl, cover and leave in a warm place to prove until doubled in size, about 30–40 minutes.

Meanwhile to make the topping, heat the oil in a pan. Add the aubergine and fry for 3 minutes. Add the pepper, onion, garlic and sweetcorn kernels. Cook over a moderate heat for 5 minutes. Add the tomatoes and salt and pepper to taste, blending well.

Knead the dough lightly into a round. Roll out on a lightly floured surface to make a 25 cm/10 inch round.

Place on a greased baking tray and spoon over the topping. Cover with the sliced cheese and garnish with a few olives.

Bake in a preheated moderate oven (180 °C, 350 °F, Gas Mark 4) for 30 minutes or until well risen and golden brown. Serve hot, cut into wedges. **Serves 4**

Above: *Vegetable and pasta stir-fry*
Below: *Vegetable pilaff*

Roulade of spinach with cheese and herbs

(Illustrated above)

Roulade
25 g/1 oz (U.S. 2 tablespoons) butter or margarine
25 g/1 oz (U.S. ¼ cup) flour
300 ml/½ pint (U.S. 1¼ cups) milk
100 g/4 oz (U.S. ½ cup) frozen leaf spinach, defrosted
and drained
salt and freshly ground black pepper
2 eggs, separated
Filling
1 × 78 g/2¾ oz packet Boursin with garlic and herbs
4 tablespoons single cream (U.S. 5 tablespoons
light cream)
6 spring onions (U.S. scallions), thinly sliced

Melt the butter in a pan. Stir in the flour and cook for
1 minute. Remove from the heat and gradually add
the milk, blending well. Bring to the boil and cook
for 2–3 minutes, stirring constantly, until smooth and
thickened.

Add the spinach, salt and pepper to taste and egg
yolks to the sauce, blending well.

Line a 15 × 28 cm/7 × 11 inch Swiss roll tin (U.S. jelly
roll pan) with greaseproof paper (U.S. waxed paper)
keeping the edges raised.

Whisk the egg whites until they stand in stiff peaks.
Fold into the sauce with a metal spoon. Pour into the
prepared tin and level the surface.

Bake in a preheated moderately hot oven (200 °C,
400 °F, Gas Mark 6) for about 10 minutes until golden
and lightly set.

Meanwhile to make the filling, mix the Boursin with
the cream and spring onions, blending well.

Turn out the roulade on to a sheet of greaseproof
paper and spread with the cheese filling. Roll up using
the paper as a guide to hold the shape. Leave to stand for
5 minutes. Serve hot, cut into slices with a tossed salad
and crusty bread.

Alternatively to serve the roulade cold, do not fill,
roll up the roulade with the paper enclosed and leave
until cold. Carefully unroll and spread with the cheese
filling. Re-roll using the paper as a guide and serve as
above. **Serves 2**

Snack bar

(Illustrated above)

250 g/9 oz (U.S. 1⅔ cups) cooked long-grain rice
100 g/4 oz (U.S. 1 cup) Edam cheese, grated
50 g/2 oz (U.S. ½ cup) ground almonds
1 teaspoon mustard powder
100 g/4 oz (U.S. ⅔ cup) seedless raisins
75 g/3 oz (U.S. 6 tablespoons) butter or margarine, melted
150 ml/¼ pint (U.S. ⅔ cup) natural yogurt
1 large egg (sizes 1, 2), beaten
75 g/3 oz (U.S. 3 cups) cornflakes

Mix the rice with the cheese, almonds, mustard and raisins, blending well.

Blend the butter or margarine with the yogurt and egg. Stir in the rice mixture and cornflakes. Press into a lightly oiled 28 × 18 cm/11 × 7 inch Swiss roll tin (U.S. jelly roll pan).

Bake in a preheated moderate oven (180 °C, 350 °F, Gas Mark 4) for 25 minutes.

While still hot, cut into about 10–12 finger slices, using a sharp knife. Leave to cool in the tin. Remove with a palette knife (U.S. spatula). **Makes 10–12 slices**

Wheatmeal cheese crown lunch loaf

1 × 280 g/11 oz packet wheatmeal bread mix
150 g/5 oz blue cheese, crumbled
1 tablespoon chopped fresh herbs
200 ml/7 fl oz (U.S. ⅞ cup) hand-hot water

Place the bread mix in a bowl with about half of the cheese and the herbs. Stir in the water and mix to form a dough. Turn on to a lightly floured surface and knead until smooth and elastic, about 5 minutes.

Divide the dough into 8 equal sized pieces and shape each piece into a round roll. Arrange in a 19 cm/7½ inch greased deep sandwich tin (U.S. deep layer cake pan), with 7 rolls around the outer edge and 1 roll in the centre.

Use a thumb to make an indent or hollow in each roll and fill with the remaining crumbled cheese. Cover and leave to prove and rise in a warm place until doubled in size, about 40 minutes.

Bake in a preheated hot oven (230 °C, 450 °F, Gas Mark 8) for about 40 minutes. Serve warm with soup, if liked. **Serves 4–6**

Sauces, dressings and stuffings

Velvety smooth, chunky and textured, light and refreshing, nutty and fruity or creamy and satisfying – there are sauce, dressing, relish and stuffing recipes here to suit all food types and meals.

Fill a shiny traffic-light coloured pepper, tomato, aubergine or courgette with a wholesome brown rice mixture; toss an assortment of leafy salad greenery in a light, clear tomato and mixed herb dressing; pile a spoonful of exotic, seemingly sun-soaked Mediterranean relish on to a hot jacket baked potato; or drizzle a stream of scrumptious addictive carob sauce over scoops of plain or fruited ice-cream.

The selection of relishes is particularly extensive in this section since they prove to be so versatile and lend themselves to so many meal-time uses. Many will cheer up a simple wedge of cheese with bread and salad for a ploughman's lunch; add a lift to baked items like flans, quiches and savoury pasties; make a splendid dip for chunky fresh vegetable crudités; and make a delicious binding dressing for potato, pasta and rice salads.

The sauces are more of the indispensable basic variety but the variations offer more scope for unusual flavours and will prove a good springboard for your own ideas – they are also called upon frequently in other recipe sections.

For convenience make sauces, stuffings, relishes and dressings in bulk and freeze or chill for speedy access. Many sauces and stuffings will freeze for up to 3 months and dressings will keep for 4 days plus in a screw-topped jar in the refrigerator.

Above left: Brown rice stuffing (recipe page 84)
Right: Tomato and mushroom sauce (recipe page 84)
Below: Cheesy garlic and herb dressing (recipe page 87)

Brown rice stuffing

(Illustrated on pages 82–83)

150 g/5 oz (U.S. ¾ cup) long-grain brown rice
225 g/8 oz (U.S. 1 cup) tomatoes, skinned, seeded
and chopped
50 g/2 oz (U.S. ½ cup) toasted hazelnuts, chopped
50 g/2 oz (U.S. ½ cup) roasted peanuts, chopped
½ teaspoon dried basil
¼ teaspoon dried oregano
1 teaspoon turmeric
salt and freshly ground black pepper
50 g/2 oz (U.S. ¼ cup) butter, melted

Cook the rice in a pan of boiling salted water until
tender, according to the packet instructions, about 20–25
minutes.

Drain the rice, rinse and place in a bowl. Add the
tomatoes, hazelnuts, peanuts, basil, oregano, turmeric
and salt and pepper to taste, blending well.

Use to stuff tomatoes, onions, peppers, aubergines (U.S.
eggplants) or courgettes (U.S. zucchini) as liked. Pour
over the melted butter and bake until the vegetables are
tender. **Serves 4**

Tomato and mushroom sauce

(Illustrated on pages 82–83)

4 teaspoons oil
1 onion, peeled and chopped
1 garlic clove, peeled and crushed
1 × 398 g/14 oz can crushed tomatoes or 450 g/1 lb
ripe tomatoes, skinned, seeded and chopped
1 × 141 g/5 oz can tomato purée
4 tablespoons (U.S. 5 tablespoons) red wine or
vegetable stock
1 tablespoon brown sugar
1 teaspoon Worcestershire sauce
½ teaspoon dried oregano
½ teaspoon dried basil
salt and freshly ground black pepper
175 g/6 oz (U.S. 1½–2 cups) cooked sliced
mushrooms

Heat the oil in a pan. Add the onion and garlic and cook
gently until softened, about 6–8 minutes.

Add the tomatoes, tomato purée, wine or stock,
sugar, Worcestershire sauce, oregano, basil and salt and
pepper to taste, blending well. Cook over a gentle heat
until thick and pulpy, about 20–25 minutes.

Stir in the mushrooms and heat through to serve.
Delicious served hot over cooked pasta.
Makes about 450 ml/¾ pint (U.S. 2 cups)

White béchamel sauce

(Illustrated opposite)

1 small onion, peeled
6 cloves
6 peppercorns
1 bay leaf
1 small carrot, peeled
300 ml/½ pint (U.S. 1¼ cups) milk
25 g/1 oz (U.S. 2 tablespoons) butter
25 g/1 oz (U.S. ¼ cup) unbleached white or
wholewheat flour
salt and freshly ground black pepper

Place the onion, cloves, peppercorns, bay leaf, carrot
and milk in a pan. Bring to the boil then remove from
the heat, cover and leave to stand for 10 minutes. Strain
into a jug.

Melt the butter in a pan. Stir in the flour and cook for
1 minute. Remove from the heat and gradually add the
strained milk, blending well. Bring to the boil and cook
for 2–3 minutes, stirring constantly, until smooth and
thickened.

Season to taste with salt and pepper and use as required.
Makes 300 ml/½ pint (U.S. 1¼ cups)

Variations
Cheese or mornay sauce Prepare and cook as above
but add 1 egg yolk mixed with 2 tablespoons double
cream (U.S. heavy cream) and 50 g/2 oz grated mature
Cheddar cheese (U.S. ½ cup grated sharp Cheddar cheese)
to the hot sauce. Stir until the cheese melts and the sauce
is smooth.
Aurore sauce Prepare and cook as above but add 2
tablespoons tomato purée and ½ teaspoon sugar to the
sauce before serving.
Parsley or herb sauce Prepare and cook as above but
add 1–2 tablespoons chopped fresh parsley or other herb
to the sauce before serving.

Above left: Carob sauce
Above right: White béchamel sauce
Below: Onion yogurt sauce

Onion yogurt sauce

(Illustrated above)

15 g/½ oz (U.S. 1 tablespoon) butter
1 small onion, peeled and finely chopped
¼ teaspoon paprika
¼ teaspoon ground coriander
salt and freshly ground black pepper
150 ml/¼ pint (U.S. ⅔ cup) natural yogurt
1 tablespoon snipped chives (optional)

Melt the butter in a small pan. Add the onion and cook gently until softened, about 6–8 minutes.

Stir in the paprika, coriander and salt and pepper to taste, blending well.

Allow to cool slightly then stir in the yogurt and chives, if used. Mix well to blend and serve at once.
Makes about 200 ml/7 fl oz (U.S. scant 1 cup)

Carob sauce

(Illustrated above)

50 g/2 oz (U.S. ¼ cup) butter
25 g/1 oz (U.S. ¼ cup) carob powder
1 egg
½ teaspoon vanilla essence (U.S. vanilla extract)
2 tablespoons golden (U.S. light corn syrup) or
maple syrup

Melt the butter in a pan. Add the carob powder, blending well.

Whisk in the egg, vanilla essence and syrup. Cook over a gentle heat, stirring constantly until the sauce thickens to a coating consistency, for about 10 minutes.

Serve warm as an alternative to chocolate sauce with ice-cream, cooked fruit such as pears or other dessert dishes. **Serves 4**

Tofu dressing

(Illustrated below)

175 g/6 oz tofu
2 tablespoons lemon juice
$3\frac{1}{2}$ tablespoons (U.S. 4 tablespoons) corn oil
$\frac{1}{2}$ teaspoon salt

Place all the ingredients in a blender and purée until smooth and creamy. Chill lightly before using.

For a thicker dressing, reduce the amount of oil.
Serves 4

Variations

Garlic and dill tofu dressing Add $\frac{1}{2}$–1 clove crushed garlic and $\frac{1}{4}$ teaspoon chopped dill.
Curry tofu dressing Add $\frac{1}{2}$ teaspoon curry powder and 2 tablespoons minced onion.
Cheese and garlic tofu dressing Add 25 g/1 oz (U.S. $\frac{1}{4}$ cup) grated Parmesan cheese or other hard cheese and $\frac{1}{2}$ clove crushed garlic. Add chopped parsley if liked.
Avocado tofu dressing Mash 1 small peeled and stoned ripe avocado and add to the dressing with a few drops of Tabasco sauce (U.S. hot pepper sauce) and 2 tablespoons minced onion.
Roquefort tofu dressing Add 1 tablespoon Roquefort cheese, $\frac{1}{2}$ clove crushed garlic and $\frac{1}{4}$ teaspoon made mustard and blend with basic dressing until smooth.

Cream cheese and chive yogonaise

(Illustrated below)

50 ml/2 fl oz (U.S. $\frac{1}{4}$ cup) natural yogurt
50 g/2 oz (U.S. $\frac{1}{4}$ cup) mayonnaise
75 g/3 oz (U.S. $\frac{1}{3}$ cup) cream cheese
2 teaspoons snipped chives
1 teaspoon lemon juice
salt and freshly ground black pepper

Mix the yogurt with the mayonnaise, cream cheese, chives and lemon juice, blending well.

Season to taste with salt and pepper. Chill lightly before serving. **Serves 4–6**

Left: *Tofu dressing*
Below: *Creamy cheese and chive yogonaise*
Below right: *Cheesy garlic and herb dressing*
Above right: *Tomato and herb dressing*

Tomato and herb dressing

(Illustrated right)

150 ml/¼ pint (U.S. ⅔ cup) tomato juice
¼ onion, peeled and grated or finely chopped
2 teaspoons chopped fresh herbs
1 small garlic clove, peeled and crushed (optional)
salt and freshly ground black pepper

Mix the tomato juice with the onion, herbs and garlic, if used, blending well.

Season to taste with salt and pepper. Chill lightly before serving. **Serves 4–6**

Cheesy garlic and herb dressing

(Illustrated below and on pages 82–83)

1 × 78 g/2¾ oz packet Boursin with garlic and herbs
3 tablespoons (U.S. 4 tablespoons) milk
1–2 teaspoons lemon juice
salt and freshly ground black pepper

Cream the cheese with the milk until smooth. Add the lemon juice and salt and pepper to taste, blending well. A delicious dressing alternative to mayonnaise. **Serves 4**

Creamy sweetcorn and celery relish

(Illustrated opposite)

100 g/4 oz (U.S. ½ cup) mayonnaise
3 tablespoons double cream (U.S. 4 tablespoons heavy cream)
2½ tablespoons sweetcorn kernels (U.S. 3 tablespoons whole kernel corn)
1 stalk celery, scrubbed and finely chopped
salt and freshly ground black pepper
celery leaves to garnish

Mix the mayonnaise with the cream, sweetcorn and celery, blending well.
    Season to taste with salt and pepper. Garnish and chill lightly before serving. **Serves 4–6**

Beetroot and apple relish

(Illustrated opposite)

150 g/5 oz (U.S. ⅔ cup) mayonnaise
75 g/3 oz cooked beetroot, peeled and finely chopped (U.S. ½ cup finely chopped cooked beet)
3 tablespoons apple purée (U.S. 4 tablespoons applesauce)
1 tablespoon finely chopped walnuts
salt and freshly ground black pepper

Mix the mayonnaise with the beetroot, apple purée and walnuts, blending well.
    Season to taste with salt and pepper. Chill lightly before serving. **Serves 4–6**

Mediterranean relish

(Illustrated opposite)

150 g/5 oz (U.S. ⅔ cup) mayonnaise
2 teaspoons lemon juice
2 tomatoes, skinned, seeded and chopped
¼ small onion, peeled and thinly sliced
3 stoned black olives (U.S. 3 pitted ripe olives), chopped
1 tablespoon finely chopped fresh parsley
salt and freshly ground black pepper

Mix the mayonnaise with the lemon juice, tomatoes, onion, olives and parsley, blending well.
    Season to taste with salt and pepper. Chill lightly before serving. **Serves 4–6**

Thick Waldorf relish

(Illustrated opposite)

8 tablespoons (U.S. 9 tablespoons) mayonnaise
1 stalk celery, scrubbed and finely chopped
¼ dessert apple, very finely chopped
1½ tablespoons unsalted roast peanuts, chopped
1 tablespoon sultanas (U.S. golden raisins)
1 tablespoon chopped walnuts
salt and freshly ground black pepper

Mix the mayonnaise with the celery, apple, peanuts, sultanas and walnuts, blending well.
    Season to taste with salt and pepper. Chill lightly before serving. **Serves 4–6**

Chilli bean relish

(Illustrated opposite)

75 g/3 oz (U.S. ⅓ cup) mayonnaise
75 g/3 oz (U.S. ½ cup) cooked red kidney beans
¼–½ teaspoon mild chilli powder (U.S. chili powder)
40 g/1½ oz (U.S. ⅓ cup) red pepper, chopped
salt and freshly ground black pepper

Mix the mayonnaise with the red kidney beans, chilli powder and red pepper, blending well.
    Season to taste with salt and pepper. Chill lightly before serving. **Serves 4–6**

Peanut relish

(Illustrated opposite)

150 g/5 oz (U.S. ⅔ cup) mayonnaise
50 g/2 oz (U.S. ½ cup) unsalted roast peanuts, chopped
25 g/1 oz (U.S. ¼ cup) carrot, finely chopped
50 g/2 oz (U.S. ½ cup) raw cauliflower, chopped
salt and freshly ground black pepper

Mix the mayonnaise with the peanuts, carrot and cauliflower, blending well.
    Season to taste with salt and pepper. Chill lightly before serving. **Serves 4–6**

From the top: *Creamy sweetcorn and celery relish, Thick Waldorf relish, Beetroot and apple relish, Chilli bean relish, Peanut relish, Mediterranean relish*

88

Accompanying vegetables and salads

Few one-pot dishes can stand alone and satisfy a main meal appetite – most dishes rely upon and are enhanced by the inclusion of a tasty crisp side salad or selection of complementary vegetables. This is still the case with vegetarian menus where main course dishes rely heavily upon the very same vegetables one associates with accompaniments.

However, a good well-balanced meal dictates variety in flavour, texture, colour and presentation, and side salads and vegetables afford such attributes. Guidelines for choice are scarce in this section since a decision will be governed by the main course dish itself, its components, its lightness or heaviness and flavour, but in general choose a light crisp side salad tossed in a dressing that will enhance rather than overpower a main course dish that is of the weighty and satisfying category, and extend a light main course dish with an imaginative selection of vegetables that add interest with each choice. Try some vegetables plain steamed, others creamed and gratinéed, with yet others that may have been baked, roasted or fried for variety.

Always prepare salads and vegetables at the last possible moment since it is within this area that freshness really counts and upon which many dishes are judged. Few guests can ever remember with accuracy a well-cooked main dish but everyone can reflect upon the limp salad or over-cooked grey soggy vegetables with unnerving pin-point clarity – it is often upon such humble beginnings that reputations can be won or lost. Ensure yours is a worthy reputation by paying attention to detail for such complementary salad and vegetable offerings.

Above left: *Aubergines with mustard (recipe page 92)*
Above right: *Crispy orange salad (recipe page 101)*
Below left: *Sweet potatoes with orange (recipe page 92)*
Below right: *Crunchy vegetable and cheese salad (recipe page 101)*

Potato layer bake

(Illustrated opposite)

900 g/2 lb potatoes, peeled and thinly sliced
1 onion, peeled and thinly sliced
175 g/6 oz (U.S. 1½ cups) Cheddar cheese, grated
50 g/2 oz (U.S. ¼ cup) butter
300 ml/½ pint (U.S. 1¼ cups) milk
salt and freshly ground black pepper
chopped fresh parsley to garnish

Layer the potatoes, onion and cheese in an ovenproof dish, dotting between each layer with a little of the butter.

Mix the milk with salt and pepper to taste and pour over the potato mixture.

Cook in a preheated moderately hot oven (190°C, 375°F, Gas Mark 5) for 1½ hours or until the potatoes are tender and golden brown. Sprinkle with chopped parsley to serve. **Serves 4**

Sweet potatoes with orange

(Illustrated on pages 90–91)

450 g/1 lb sweet potatoes, scrubbed
65 g/2½ oz (U.S. 5 tablespoons) butter
freshly ground black pepper
5 tablespoons (U.S. 6 tablespoons) orange syrup
½ teaspoon ground cinnamon
To garnish
chopped fresh parsley
orange rind strips (optional)

Cook the potatoes in their skins in a pan of boiling water for 30 minutes or until tender. Drain and when cool enough to handle, peel off the skins. Cut the flesh into bite-sized chunks.

Melt the butter in a pan. Add the sweet potato chunks, pepper to taste, orange syrup and cinnamon, blending well.

Cook over a gentle heat, stirring occasionally, until the potatoes are glazed and the liquid has evaporated.

Spoon into a warmed serving dish and sprinkle with chopped parsley to serve. **Serves 4**

Aubergines with mustard

(Illustrated on pages 90–91)

50 g/2 oz (U.S. ¼ cup) butter
1 tablespoon oil
450 g/1 lb aubergines (U.S. eggplants)
1 tablespoon wholegrain mustard
salt and freshly ground black pepper
To garnish
chopped fresh parsley
fresh herb sprig

Place the butter and oil in a large shallow ovenproof dish. Cook in a preheated moderately hot oven (200°C, 400°F, Gas Mark 6) for 5 minutes until hot and melted.

Meanwhile, cut the stalks off the aubergines and slice lengthwise into quarters. Spread with the mustard and add salt and pepper to taste.

Place the aubergine pieces, skin side down, in the hot fat. Bake for 30 minutes, turning over halfway through the cooking time. Serve hot. **Serves 4**

Variations
Aubergines with horseradish mustard Prepare and cook as above but mix the wholegrain mustard with ½ teaspoon grated fresh horseradish or 1 teaspoon made horseradish sauce or relish.
Aubergines with herbed mustard Prepare and cook as above but mix the wholegrain mustard with 1 teaspoon snipped chives or other chopped mixed herbs to taste. Use herbs that will complement the main course dish you intend to serve the aubergines with.
Aubergines with onion and mustard Prepare and cook as above but mix the wholegrain mustard with 2 teaspoons grated onion or 2 teaspoons snipped spring onion (U.S. scallion) tops.

Potato layer bake

Celery with Stilton and port sauce

(Illustrated above)

6 stalks celery, scrubbed
40 g/1½ oz (U.S. 3 tablespoons) butter
40 g/1½ oz (U.S. 6 tablespoons) white or wholewheat flour
300 ml/½ pint (U.S. 1¼ cups) milk
salt and freshly ground black pepper
100 g/4 oz (U.S. 1 cup) white Stilton cheese, grated
3 tablespoons (U.S. 4 tablespoons) port

Cut the celery into 2.5 cm/1 inch lengths. Cook in a pan of boiling salted water until tender, about 10 minutes.

Meanwhile, melt the butter in a pan. Stir in the flour and cook for 1 minute. Remove from the heat and gradually add the milk, blending well. Bring to the boil and cook for 2 minutes, stirring constantly, until smooth and thickened. Season to taste with salt and pepper.

Add the cheese to the sauce and stir until melted. Remove from the heat and stir in the port, blending well.

Drain the celery and place in a flameproof dish. Spoon over the sauce and brown under a preheated hot grill (U.S. broiler). **Serves 4–6**

Variations
Fennel with Stilton and port sauce Prepare and cook as above but use 2 small bulbs of fennel instead of the celery. Slice the stalks into rings and cut the bulbs into quarters. Cook in boiling salted water for about 10–15 minutes, until tender.
Celery and artichokes with Stilton and port sauce Prepare and cook as above but add 1 × 200 g/7 oz can drained and halved artichokes in brine to the cooked celery, mix well then place in an ovenproof dish. Cover with the prepared sauce and cook under a preheated grill (U.S. broiler) until golden and bubbly, and the artichokes are warmed through.

Mushroom slaw

(Illustrated above)

225 g/8 oz (U.S. 2 cups) open cup mushrooms,
wiped and sliced
225 g/8 oz (U.S. 3 cups) white cabbage,
shredded
50 g/2 oz sultanas (U.S. $\frac{1}{3}$ cup golden raisins)
Dressing
150 ml/$\frac{1}{4}$ pint (U.S. $\frac{2}{3}$ cup) mayonnaise
2 tablespoons lemon juice
2 tablespoons Dijon mustard
2 tablespoons single cream (U.S. light cream)
2 tablespoons snipped chives
salt and freshly ground black pepper

Place the mushrooms in a bowl and add the cabbage and
sultanas, blending well.

To make the dressing, blend the mayonnaise with the
lemon juice, mustard, cream, chives and salt and pepper
to taste.

Pour over the mushroom mixture and toss gently to
mix. Cover and chill for 3–4 hours before serving.
Serves 6

Spiced coleslaw

450 g/1 lb white cabbage (or a mixture of red
and white cabbage)
1 large onion, peeled and grated
2 carrots, peeled and grated
2 dessert apples, grated
50 g/2 oz (U.S. $\frac{1}{2}$ cup) broken walnuts
75 g/3 oz (U.S. $\frac{1}{2}$ cup) mixed dried fruit (e.g. apricots,
raisins, prunes and dates), chopped
4–5 tablespoons (U.S. 5–6 tablespoons) curry-flavoured
mayonnaise
chopped fresh parsley to garnish

Core and finely shred the cabbage into a large bowl.
Add the onion, carrots, apple, walnuts and fruit, blending
well.

Spoon over the curry-flavoured mayonnaise and toss
gently to coat. Serve lightly chilled, sprinkled with
chopped parsley. **Serves 6**

Caesar bean salad

(Illustrated below)

1 × 450 g/1 lb can baked beans
juice of ½ lemon
salt and freshly ground black pepper
2 teaspoons Worcestershire sauce
2 garlic cloves, peeled and crushed
1 egg
5 tablespoons (U.S. 6 tablespoons) olive oil
2 slices bread, cubed
1 small iceberg lettuce, shredded
1 head chicory (U.S. endive), shredded
75 g/3 oz (U.S. ½ cup) cooked French beans
12 black olives (U.S. ripe olives)
chopped parsley or snipped chives to garnish

Drain the beans thoroughly in a sieve over a bowl. Mix the bean juice with the lemon juice, salt and pepper to taste, Worcestershire sauce and half of the garlic.

Soft boil the egg in a pan of boiling water for ¾ minute. Crack the shell carefully and scoop the liquid egg into the dressing. Beat well with a fork, adding 2 tablespoons of the oil.

Heat the remaining oil in a shallow pan. Add the remaining garlic and the bread cubes and fry until crisp and golden. Drain on absorbent kitchen towel.

Place the lettuce, chicory, French beans and olives in a serving bowl. Add the drained baked beans and croûtons and mix gently.

Add the prepared dressing and toss gently to mix. Sprinkle with chopped parsley or snipped chives and serve at once. **Serves 4**

Below: *Caesar bean salad*
Right: *Waldorf bean salad*

Waldorf bean salad

(Illustrated below)

1 × 450 g/1 lb can barbecue beans
3 tablespoons (U.S. 4 tablespoons) olive oil
salt and freshly ground black pepper
1 garlic clove, peeled and crushed
1 tablespoon chopped fresh mint
3 stalks celery, scrubbed and sliced
100 g/4 oz (U.S. 1 cup) green beans, trimmed
2 tablespoons coarsely chopped walnuts
1 large lettuce heart, quartered
1 red dessert apple, cored and sliced
1 teaspoon lemon juice

Drain the beans thoroughly in a sieve. Mix the bean juice with the oil, salt and pepper to taste, garlic and half of the mint, blending well.

Mix the drained beans with the celery, green beans, half of the walnuts and a little of the prepared dressing.

Arrange the lettuce heart on a serving dish. Toss the apple slices in the lemon juice to prevent browning and arrange around the lettuce.

Spoon the barbecue bean mixture on top of the lettuce and spoon over the remaining dressing. Sprinkle with the remaining walnuts and mint. Serve at once. **Serves 4**

Apple, avocado and celery pasta salad

(Illustrated above and on the front cover)

225 g/8 oz (U.S. 2 cups) pasta shapes (e.g. bows,
rings, wheels, shells, twists or bows)
1 avocado, peeled, stoned and sliced
1 red dessert apple, cored and sliced
2 teaspoons lemon juice
3 stalks celery, scrubbed and chopped
4 tablespoons (U.S. 5 tablespoons) French dressing
salt and freshly ground black pepper

Cook the pasta in a pan of boiling salted water until
tender or 'al dente' according to the packet instructions.
Drain and refresh under cold water.

Mix the avocado and apple slices with the lemon juice
to prevent browning.

Place the cooked pasta, avocado and apple, celery,
dressing and salt and pepper to taste in a serving bowl.
Toss gently to mix before serving. **Serves 4**

George Cave salad

4 George Cave or other crisp dessert apples
3 heads chicory (U.S. endive)
1 celery heart, chopped
1 small red or green pepper, seeded and chopped
100 g/4 oz (U.S. ½ cup) cream cheese
16 walnut halves
paprika
150 ml/¼ pint (U.S. ⅔ cup) soured cream or yogurt
1 teaspoon sugar
2–4 teaspoons tarragon vinegar or lemon juice
1 teaspoon French mustard
salt and freshly ground black pepper
lemon juice

Peel, core and chop three of the apples, place in a
bowl. Peel the outer leaves from the chicory, rinse and
use to line the outer edge of a serving dish. Slice the
remaining chicory and add to the chopped apple with
the celery heart and pepper.

Divide the cream cheese into about eight portions,
using a teaspoon, and roll into small balls. Press a walnut
half on each side and dust the cheese with paprika.

To make the dressing, beat the soured cream or yogurt
with the sugar, tarragon vinegar or lemon juice to taste
and mustard, blending well. Season to taste.

Add the dressing to the chopped apple mixture and
toss to coat. Spoon into the centre of the chicory-lined
serving dish. Arrange the cheese balls around the salad.

Core and slice the remaining apple and dip in lemon
juice. Use to garnish the salad. **Serves 4**

Orange, spinach and mushroom salad

(Illustrated above)

6 thick slices bread, cubed
oil for frying
450 g/1 lb young spinach leaves, washed
100 g/4 oz (U.S. 1 cup) mushrooms, wiped and
sliced
3 oranges, peeled, pith removed and cut into
segments
radicchio leaves
Dressing
50 g/2 oz (U.S. $\frac{1}{3}$ cup) blue cheese
2 tablespoons olive oil
grated rind and juice of 1 orange
1 tablespoon chopped fresh parsley
salt and freshly ground black pepper

Heat about 5 mm/$\frac{1}{4}$ inch oil in a frying pan (U.S. skillet). Add the bread cubes and fry until crisp and golden. Drain on absorbent kitchen towel.

Mix the spinach with the mushrooms, oranges and fried croûtons, blending well.

Line a serving dish with radicchio leaves and pile the spinach salad mixture on top.

To make the dressing, place the cheese, oil, orange rind, orange juice, parsley and salt and pepper to taste in a blender or food processor. Blend for 30 seconds. Pour over the salad or serve separately. **Serves 4**

Mushroom bean salad

(Illustrated above)

350 g/12 oz (U.S. 2 cups) cooked flageolet beans
450 g/1 lb (U.S. 4 cups) small button mushrooms,
wiped and trimmed
$\frac{1}{2}$ red pepper, cored, seeded and finely chopped
4 spring onions (U.S. scallions), trimmed and
chopped
Dressing
175 ml/6 fl oz (U.S. $\frac{3}{4}$ cup) natural yogurt
5 tablespoons (U.S. $\frac{1}{3}$ cup) mayonnaise
2 tablespoons snipped chives
salt and freshly ground black pepper
spring onion (U.S. scallion) tassels to garnish

Mix the flageolet beans with the mushrooms, red pepper and spring onions in a serving bowl.

To make the dressing, mix the yogurt with the mayonnaise, half of the chives and salt and pepper to taste, blending well.

Drizzle the dressing over the salad and chill until required. Serve the salad sprinkled with the remaining chives, then garnish. **Serves 4**

Crispy orange salad

(Illustrated on pages 90–91)

4 oranges, peeled, pith removed and segmented
1 × 425 g/15 oz can red kidney beans, drained
225 g/8 oz (U.S. 4 cups) beansprouts, sorted
4 stalks celery, scrubbed and chopped
2 tablespoons French dressing
1 tablespoon chopped fresh parsley
salt and freshly ground black pepper

Mix the orange segments with the beans, beansprouts and celery in a bowl.

Mix the French dressing with the parsley and salt and pepper to taste, blending well.

Pour over the salad and toss gently to mix. Serve at once. **Serves 4–6**

Crunchy vegetable and cheese salad

(Illustrated on pages 90–91)

75 g/3 oz French beans (U.S. ¾ cup green beans), trimmed
1 head fennel, cut into thin julienne strips
100 g/4 oz (U.S. ½ cup) carrots, peeled and cut into thin julienne strips
½ small cauliflower, divided into small florets
1 courgette (U.S. zucchini), trimmed and very thinly sliced
4 tablespoons (U.S. 5 tablespoons) Cream Cheese and Chive Yogonaise (see page 86)
salt and freshly ground black pepper

Cook the beans in a pan of boiling salted water for 2–3 minutes. Drain and cool in iced water.

Drain the beans. Mix with the fennel, carrots, cauliflower, courgette, dressing and salt and pepper to taste, blending well.

Chill lightly before serving as a side salad. **Serves 4**

Aubergine fritters

(Illustrated opposite)

2–3 aubergines (U.S. eggplants), sliced
salt
100 g/4 oz plain flour (U.S. 1 cup all-purpose flour)
¼ teaspoon cayenne pepper
2 eggs, beaten
150 ml/¼ pint (U.S. ⅔ cup) milk
oil for deep frying
lemon wedges to garnish

Place the aubergine slices in a colander, sprinkle with salt and leave to drain for 10 minutes. Rinse and dry thoroughly.

Meanwhile, mix the flour with the cayenne pepper in a bowl. Make a well in the centre, add the eggs and gradually beat into the flour, adding the milk to make a smooth batter. Add the aubergine slices, cover and leave to stand for 15 minutes.

Heat the oil in a pan to 190°C/375°F or until a cube of bread browns in 1 minute. Add the aubergine slices, one at a time, and fry until golden, about 3 minutes. Drain on absorbent kitchen towel.

Serve at once as a vegetable dish or starter. Garnish with lemon wedges and serve with tartare sauce if liked. **Serves 4**

Chinese fried vegetables

3 tablespoons (U.S. 4 tablespoons) oil
1 garlic clove, peeled and crushed
2.5 cm/1 inch piece fresh root ginger, peeled and thinly sliced
salt and freshly ground black pepper
2 carrots, peeled and thinly sliced
1 red or green pepper, cored, seeded and sliced into thin strips
1 small cauliflower, broken into small florets
50 g/2 oz (U.S. 1 cup) beansprouts
75 ml/3 fl oz (U.S. ½ cup) vegetable stock
3 tablespoons (U.S. 4 tablespoons) orange juice
2 teaspoons soy sauce
1 teaspoon soft brown sugar

Heat the oil in a large frying pan (U.S. skillet). When hot, add the garlic, ginger and salt and pepper to taste and stir-fry for 1 minute.

Add the carrots and stir-fry for 1 minute. Stir in the pepper and cauliflower and stir-fry for a further 3 minutes. Add the beansprouts and stir-fry for 1 minute.

Stir in the stock, orange juice, soy sauce and brown sugar. Cover and cook for 3–4 minutes or until the vegetables are just tender but still crisp.

Transfer to a warmed serving dish and serve at once. **Serves 4**

Aubergine fritters

Children's vegetarian dishes

Few groups of people are more susceptible to the maladies of an unbalanced diet than children – too few or too many ill-assorted and unbalanced nutrients presented at a time when requirements are extra high serve to highlight the dangers of many imperfect meals. It is currently fashionable to restrict the meat intake, especially red meat intake, of a child's diet in an attempt to reduce fats, lower meat-fattening hormone levels and by doing so increase fibre, vitamin and mineral intake. It is a trend to applaud and approve when there is a growing danger of a nation of children being brought up on additive-laden, fat-rich and artificially-colour-intensified food.

Fortunately the early years of a child's life are the perfect time to set down and establish a pattern of eating for life. Present a pre-school child with delicious fruit, vegetable, cereal and nut dishes as a matter of course and judiciously limit sweeter confections and it is often true there are fewer problems to face in the later school and teenage years on the food front.

Vegetarian food for children should however still be fun so presentation is still important to ensure eye appeal – Bean Rafts and Energy Wedges are two recipes in this section that illustrate how easy it is to make nutritious wholesome cereals and pulses attractive enough for children to want, not just need, to eat.

Above left: *Herby vegetable tart (recipe page 104)*
Above right: *Cheesy crust toasties (recipe page 104)*
Below: *Hot apple muffins (recipe page 108)*

Cheesy crust toasties

(Illustrated on pages 102–103)

crusts cut from a large wholewheat tin loaf
50 g/2 oz (U.S. ¼ cup) butter
175 g/6 oz (U.S. 1½ cups) Cheddar cheese, grated
5 tomatoes
1 × 335 g/11.8 oz can sweetcorn kernels (U.S. whole
kernel corn), drained

Spread the bread crusts (four long pieces and two ends) with the butter and sprinkle with half of the cheese. Coarsely chop two of the tomatoes, thinly slice the remainder.

Top the crusts with the sweetcorn kernels and chopped tomatoes. Cover with the remaining cheese and sliced tomatoes.

Cook under a preheated low to medium grill (U.S. broiler) until the filling is hot, bubbly and golden, about 8–10 minutes.

Serve hot, cut into manageable pieces, with paper napkins. **Serves 4–6**

Herby vegetable tart

(Illustrated on pages 102–103)

Base
175 g/6 oz (U.S. 1½ cups) plain wholewheat flour
pinch of salt
75 g/3 oz (U.S. 6 tablespoons) butter or margarine
about 2–3 tablespoons cold water
Filling
2 carrots, peeled and thinly sliced
½ small cauliflower, divided into small florets
25 g/1 oz (U.S. 2 tablespoons) butter
25 g/1 oz (U.S. ¼ cup) flour
250 ml/8 fl oz (U.S. 1 cup) milk
1 × 340 g/12 oz can sweetcorn kernels (U.S. whole
kernel corn), drained
2 eggs, beaten
2 tablespoons chopped fresh herbs
salt and freshly ground black pepper
2 tablespoons grated Parmesan or Cheddar
cheese

To make the pastry, mix the flour with the salt in a bowl. Rub in (U.S. cut in) the butter or margarine until the mixture resembles fine breadcrumbs. Add the water and bind to a firm but pliable dough.

Roll out pastry on floured surface to a round large enough to line a 20 cm/8 inch flan tin. Prick base, line with greaseproof paper (U.S. waxed paper), fill with baking beans. Bake blind in a preheated moderately hot oven (200°C, 400°F, Gas Mark 6) for 10 minutes. Remove beans and paper and bake for a further 5 minutes.

Meanwhile to make the filling, cook the carrots and cauliflower in a pan of boiling salted water for 4 minutes. Drain, rinse in cold water and drain again.

Melt the butter in a pan. Stir in the flour and cook for 1 minute. Remove from the heat and gradually add the milk, blending well. Bring to the boil and cook for 2–3 minutes, stirring constantly, until smooth and thickened. Remove from the heat, add the sweetcorn, eggs and herbs, blending well.

Fold in the carrots and cauliflower with salt and pepper to taste. Spoon into the partly cooked pastry case and sprinkle with the cheese.

Return to the oven and bake until set and golden, about 30–35 minutes. Serve warm or cold with a little salad. **Serves 4–6**

Vegetarian lunchbox specials

Spicy bean roll
1 wholemeal bread roll
7 g/¼ oz (U.S. ½ tablespoon) butter or margarine
100 g/4 oz (U.S. ¾ cup) baked beans in tomato sauce
1½ teaspoons sweet pickle
½ teaspoon mayonnaise
salt and freshly ground black pepper
Munchy crunch sandwich
50 g/2 oz (U.S. ¼ cup) smooth peanut butter
50 g/2 oz (U.S. ¼ cup) cream cheese
25 g/1 oz (U.S. ¼ cup) grated carrot
25 g/1 oz (U.S. ¼ cup) grated or finely chopped celery
2 slices wholewheat bread

To make the spicy bean roll, split the bread roll and spread with the butter or margarine. Mash the baked beans with the sweet pickle, mayonnaise and salt and pepper to taste. Use to fill the roll.

To make the munchy crunch sandwich, mix the peanut butter with the cream cheese, carrot, celery and salt and pepper to taste. Use to sandwich the two slices of bread together and slice in half.

Wrap both roll and sandwich in cling film (U.S. Saran wrap) or greaseproof paper (U.S. waxed paper) to transport. **Serves 1**

Cheesy courgette layer

Cheesy courgette layer

(Illustrated below)

675 g/1½ lb courgettes (U.S. zucchini), trimmed and thinly sliced
40 g/1½ oz (U.S. 3 tablespoons) butter
1 onion, peeled and chopped
1 garlic clove, peeled and crushed (optional)
1 × 398 g/14 oz can peeled tomatoes, drained and chopped
25 g/1 oz (U.S. ¼ cup) wholewheat flour
300 ml/½ pint (U.S. 1¼ cups) milk
2 tablespoons natural yogurt
175 g/6 oz (U.S. 1½ cups) Cheshire cheese, grated
50 g/2 oz (U.S. 1 cup) wholewheat breadcrumbs
fresh herb sprig to garnish

Blanch the courgettes in a pan of boiling water for 2 minutes, then drain thoroughly.

Melt half the butter in a pan. Add the onion and garlic, if used, and cook until softened, about 5 minutes. Add the tomatoes, blending well, and simmer for a further 5 minutes.

Meanwhile, place the remaining butter, flour and milk in a pan. Heat, whisking constantly, until smooth and thickened. Cook for 2 minutes, then stir in the yogurt and 100 g/4 oz (U.S. 1 cup) of the cheese, blending well.

Arrange one third of the courgettes in a greased oven-proof dish. Top with half of the tomato mixture and half of the sauce. Repeat, finishing with a layer of courgettes.

Mix the breadcrumbs with the remaining cheese and sprinkle over the courgettes. Bake in a preheated moderate oven (180°C, 350°F, Gas Mark 4) for 40 minutes. Serve hot. **Serves 4**

Bean rafts

(Illustrated opposite)

3 × 5 cm/2 inch thick slices wholewheat bread
(cut from a large uncut loaf)
melted butter or beaten egg to glaze
1 × 450 g/1 lb can baked beans in tomato
sauce
12 long thin strips cheese
fresh herb sprigs to garnish

Remove the crusts from the bread and square-up each slice. Cut each slice in half to make six rectangles measuring about 7.5 × 5 cm/3 × 2 inches. Using a small sharp knife, carefully cut out the centre of each bread rectangle leaving a 1 cm/½ inch 'wall' all the way around. Pull out the bread from the centre (use for another recipe or for making breadcrumbs). These are the bread rafts.

Brush the rafts with melted butter or beaten egg to glaze on all sides. Place on a baking tray. Bake in a preheated moderately hot oven (200°C, 400°F, Gas Mark 6) for about 15 minutes until golden.

Meanwhile, heat the beans until hot. Arrange the rafts on a serving plate and fill the centres with the hot baked beans. Position two strips of cheese in the rafts to represent 'oars'. Serve at once. **Serves 6**

Potato flappers

(Illustrated opposite)

350 g/12 oz (U.S. about 3 cups) potatoes, peeled
and grated
100 g/4 oz (U.S. 1⅓ cups) apple, grated
1 large onion, peeled and finely chopped
2 teaspoons fresh mixed dried herbs
2 eggs, beaten
50 g/2 oz (U.S. 1 cup) All Bran
salt and freshly ground black pepper
4 tablespoons (U.S. 5 tablespoons) oil
apple slices to garnish

Mix the potatoes with the apple, onion, herbs, egg, All Bran and salt and pepper to taste, blending well.

Divide the mixture into four portions. Heat 1 tablespoon of the oil in a frying pan (U.S. skillet). Add one portion of the potato mixture and fry until golden brown on the underside, about 6 minutes. Turn over and cook gently until golden on the other side and cooked through.

Drain on absorbent kitchen towel and keep warm. Repeat with the remaining mixture to make four potato flappers. Serve as a teatime treat with baked beans if liked. **Serves 4**

Crunchy apple and Cheshire flan

(Illustrated opposite)

Base
150 g/5 oz (U.S. 1¼ cups) wholewheat flour
pinch of salt
1 tablespoon brown sugar
50 g/2 oz (U.S. 2 cups) wheat flakes, lightly crushed
4 tablespoons (U.S. 5 tablespoons) oil
2–3 tablespoons water
Filling
450 g/1 lb cooking apples, peeled and cored
2 tablespoons water
1 tablespoon brown sugar
100 g/4 oz (U.S. ⅔ cup) raisins
100 g/4 oz (U.S. 1 cup) Cheshire cheese, grated

To make the base, mix the flour with the salt, sugar, wheat flakes, oil and water, blending well. Spoon into a deep 20 cm/8 inch pie plate and press evenly and firmly over the base and sides. Bake in a preheated moderately hot oven (200°C, 400°F, Gas Mark 6) for 15 minutes.

Meanwhile for the filling, coarsely chop half of the apples and place in a pan with the water and sugar. Cook gently until soft and reduced to a pulp. Cool slightly then stir in the raisins and three-quarters of the cheese, blending well. Spoon into the prepared flan case.

Slice the remaining apple into thin segments and poach in a little water until just tender. Plunge into cold water to prevent further cooking, then drain.

Arrange the apple slices in an overlapping pattern on top of the flan. Sprinkle with the remaining cheese.

Protect the flan crust with a foil rim. Place under a preheated hot grill (U.S. broiler) and cook until the cheese melts and turns a golden brown. Cool before serving. **Serves 6–8**

Above: Potato flappers
Centre: Bean rafts
Below: Crunchy apple and Cheshire flan

Hot apple muffins

(Illustrated on pages 102–103)

Base
225 g/8 oz (U.S. 2 cups) plain wholewheat flour
1 teaspoon salt
3 teaspoons baking powder
50 g/2 oz (U.S. ¼ cup) sugar
2 eggs
150 ml/¼ pint (U.S. ⅔ cup) milk
50 g/2 oz (U.S. ¼ cup) butter, melted
6 tablespoons (U.S. 7 tablespoons) chopped peeled dessert apple
Topping
4 red dessert apples, peeled, cored and thickly sliced
5 tablespoons (U.S. 6 tablespoons) sugar
2 teaspoons ground cinnamon

To make the base, mix the flour with the salt, baking powder and sugar, blending well. Beat the eggs with the milk and butter. Stir quickly into the flour mixture but do not beat. Fold in the chopped apples.

To make the topping, toss the apple slices in the sugar and cinnamon.

Grease 24 × 5 cm/2 inch bun or muffin tins and place in a preheated hot oven (220°C, 425°F, Gas Mark 7) until very hot.

Fill the bun cases a third full with the batter mixture and top with a little of the apple topping. Return to the oven and bake until well risen, cooked and golden, about 15–20 minutes.

Remove from the tins and serve hot. The muffins can also be reheated from cold by placing in a paper bag and cooking in a hot oven for 5–6 minutes. **Makes 20–24**

Coffee and walnut fudge pudding

225 g/8 oz (U.S. 1 cup) butter
275 g/10 oz (U.S. 1⅔ cups) muscovado sugar
2 eggs
6 tablespoons (U.S. 7 tablespoons) coffee and chicory essence
225 g/8 oz self-raising flour (U.S. 2 cups self-rising flour sifted with 2 teaspoons baking powder)
60 ml/2½ fl oz (U.S. ⅓ cup) milk
60 ml/2½ fl oz (U.S. ⅓ cup) oil
100 g/4 oz (U.S. 1 cup) walnuts, chopped
100 g/4 oz sultanas (U.S. ⅔ cup golden raisins)
Sauce
75 g/3 oz (U.S. 6 tablespoons) butter
150 g/5 oz (U.S. ¾ cup) muscovado sugar
4 tablespoons double cream (U.S. 5 tablespoons heavy cream)

To make the pudding, cream the butter and sugar until light and fluffy. Beat in the eggs and coffee and chicory essence, blending well. Gradually add the flour, milk and oil, beating well to make a mixture with a soft dropping consistency. Fold in the walnuts and sultanas.

Spoon into a greased 2.4 litre/4 pint (U.S. 5 pint) oven-proof dish. Bake in a preheated moderate oven (160°C, 325°F, Gas Mark 3) for 50 minutes.

To make the sauce, melt the butter in a pan. Add the sugar and bring to the boil. Stir in the cream and simmer until thickened, about 2–3 minutes. Serve the pudding hot, topped with the sauce. **Serves 6–8**

Energy wedges

(Illustrated opposite)

3 small chocolate fudge finger bars
100 g/4 oz (U.S. ½ cup) butter or margarine
1 tablespoon cocoa powder (U.S. unsweetened cocoa)
1 tablespoon milk
100 g/4 oz digestive wheatmeal biscuits (U.S. 1½ cups wholewheat graham crackers), crushed
100 g/4 oz stoned dates (U.S. ⅔ cup pitted dates), chopped
100 g/4 oz (U.S. ⅔ cup) dried peaches, chopped
50 g/2 oz (U.S. 2 cups) Start cereal

Place the fudge bars, butter or margarine, cocoa and milk in a pan. Heat gently until melted, stirring occasionally.

Add the crushed biscuits, dates and peaches, blending well.

Spoon into an 18 cm/7 inch lightly greased sandwich tin (U.S. layer cake pan) and level the surface. Decorate with the cereal. Allow to cool, then chill to set.

To serve, turn out and cut into wedges. **Makes 6 wedges**

Above: Fruity orange slice
Below: Energy wedges

Fruity orange slice

(Illustrated above)

100 g/4 oz (U.S. $\frac{1}{2}$ cup) butter or margarine
100 g/4 oz demerara sugar (U.S. $\frac{2}{3}$ cup brown
sugar)
2 eggs, beaten
100 g/4 oz self-raising flour (U.S. 1 cup self-rising
flour sifted with 1 teaspoon baking powder)
$\frac{1}{2}$ teaspoon grated nutmeg
grated rind and juice of 1 orange
100 g/4 oz (U.S. $2\frac{1}{2}$ cups) Fruit 'n Fibre cereal
5 tablespoons (U.S. 6 tablespoons) rhubarb and ginger
preserve or other preserve
icing sugar (U.S. confectioner's sugar) to dust

Cream the butter or margarine with the sugar in a bowl
until light and fluffy. Beat in the eggs, blending well.

Fold in the flour, nutmeg, orange rind, orange juice
and Fruit 'n Fibre cereal, blending well.

Spoon into a greased and base-lined 18 × 28 cm/7 × 11
inch tin, levelling the surface. Bake in a preheated moderate oven (180°C, 350°F, Gas Mark 4) for 25 minutes.
Allow to cool in the tin.

Turn out and cut into two layers. Sandwich together
again with the preserve. Dust with icing sugar and cut
into squares to serve. **Makes 1 × 18 × 28 cm/7 × 11 inch slice**

Variation
Fruity apricot slice Prepare and cook as above but
sandwich the orange layers together with a sweetened
dried apricot purée. Make by cooking 100 g/4 oz (U.S.
$\frac{2}{3}$ cup) dried apricots in a little water or fruit juice until
soft, about 30 minutes. Drain, if necessary, and mash to
a pulp or purée with 1–2 teaspoons clear honey, if liked.
Cool and use instead of preserve above.

Vegan fare

A diet without milk, butter, cheese, yogurt, honey and eggs alongside the usual vegetarian 'no-goes' seems to many like a diet that lacks variety, nourishment and indeed staying power. However to the many people who follow such a course, called vegans, it is a way of life that not only reflects their attitudes to food in the practical sense but has become a very attractive alternative that doesn't seem the slightest bit restrictive.

Consider feasting upon Chick Pea, Corn and Apple Salad, Forties Lentil Pie, Vegetable and Bean Biryani or Crunchy Vegetable Salad and you can see at a glance that such a diet has ample variety in terms of flavour and texture and many virtues in terms of nutrients.

There are ideas in this section for quick and easy speedy lunchboxes like Tuscan Bean and Nut Salad, and Mushroom and Celery Bean-feast; nourishing 'one-pot' snacks like Chilli Beansprouts; and main courses fit to serve for entertaining like Vegan Pilaff. Scattered throughout the book are also many other delicious and suitable savoury, sweet, hot, cold, breakfast, supper, main course and home-baked dishes that are vegan style.

It should be remembered however that with a restricted diet of the vegan kind that variety in nutrients is all-important to maintain good health – so make sure your vegan diet is rich in the very many different vegetable, pulse, nut, fruit and cereal ingredients on offer – taking additional dietary supplements if needed and permitted.

Above left: *Chick pea, corn and apple salad (recipe page 112)*
Above right: *Vegetable and bean biryani (recipe page 114)*
Below: *Forties lentil pie (recipe page 112)*

Chick pea, corn and apple salad

(Illustrated on pages 110–111)

450 g/1 lb cooked chick (U.S. garbanzo) peas
350 g/12 oz cooked sweetcorn kernels (U.S. 1½ cups cooked whole kernel corn)
2 stalks celery, scrubbed and chopped
1 bunch watercress, trimmed
50 g/2 oz (U.S. ½ cup) walnut pieces
2 red dessert apples, cored and sliced
1 tablespoon lemon juice
4 tablespoons (U.S. 5 tablespoons) French dressing

Place the chick peas, sweetcorn, celery, watercress and walnuts in a serving bowl.

Toss the apple slices in the lemon juice and add to the bowl.

Pour over the dressing and toss gently to mix. **Serves 4**

Forties lentil pie

(Illustrated on pages 110–111)

175 g/6 oz (U.S. ¾ cup) red lentils
1 onion, peeled and chopped
350 g/12 oz (U.S. 1½ cups) cooked potatoes, mashed
2 tablespoons chopped fresh parsley
1 × 335 g/11.8 oz can sweetcorn kernels (U.S. whole kernel corn), drained
2 tablespoons chutney
salt and freshly ground black pepper
onion rings to garnish

Rinse and place the lentils with the onion in a pan. Cover with cold water, bring to the boil, reduce the heat and simmer until tender, about 25 minutes.

Drain thoroughly and mix with the potatoes, parsley, sweetcorn, chutney and salt and pepper to taste. Spoon into a flameproof dish and cook under a preheated hot grill (U.S. broiler) until golden and crisp. Garnish and serve. **Serves 4**

Vegan pilaff

(Illustrated opposite)

4 tablespoons (U.S. 5 tablespoons) vegetable oil
1 tablespoon chopped onion
75 g/3 oz (U.S. ½ cup) dried apricots or nectarines, soaked overnight and chopped
75 g/3 oz (U.S. ½ cup) dried prunes, soaked overnight and chopped
50 g/2 oz sultanas (U.S. ⅓ cup golden raisins)
25 g/1 oz (U.S. 3 tablespoons) raisins
150 ml/¼ pint (U.S. ⅔ cup) apple or orange juice
2 large bananas, peeled and sliced
75 g/3 oz (U.S. ¾ cup) walnut pieces
25 g/1 oz (U.S. ¼–⅓ cup) pine nuts
1 tablespoon clear honey
225 g/8 oz (U.S. generous 1 cup) long-grain brown rice
450 ml/¾ pint (U.S. 2 cups) water
salt and freshly ground black pepper
1 red dessert apple, cored and chopped
To garnish
onion rings
chopped fresh parsley
lemon wedges (optional)

Heat the oil in a large pan. Add the onion and cook for 3 minutes. Add the apricots or nectarines, prunes, sultanas, raisins and apple or orange juice, blending well. Cook for 5 minutes, stirring occasionally.

Add the bananas, walnuts, pine nuts, honey, rice, water and salt and pepper to taste. Bring to the boil, reduce the heat, cover and simmer until the rice is tender, about 25–30 minutes.

Stir in the apple and cook gently to reheat. Spoon into a warmed serving dish and garnish with onion rings and chopped parsley. Serve hot. **Serves 4**

Vegan pilaff

112

Vegetable and bean biryani

(Illustrated above and pages 110–111)

1 medium aubergine (U.S. eggplant), cubed
salt and freshly ground black pepper
4 tablespoons (U.S. 5 tablespoons) vegetable oil or
vegetable ghee
$\frac{3}{4}$ teaspoon poppy seeds
1 teaspoon mustard seeds
pinch of cayenne pepper
$\frac{1}{4}$ teaspoon turmeric
$\frac{3}{4}$ teaspoon garam masala
$\frac{1}{4}$ teaspoon ground coriander
1 red pepper, cored, seeded and sliced
75 g/3 oz cooked butter beans or haricot beans
(U.S. $\frac{1}{2}$ cup cooked navy beans)
2 tomatoes, skinned, seeded and chopped
225 g/8 oz (U.S. generous 1 cup) long-grain brown
rice, cooked with a little saffron
toasted pine nuts
raisins
coriander sprig to garnish

Place the aubergine cubes in a colander, sprinkle with salt and leave for 30 minutes. Rinse the cubes and dry.

Heat the oil or ghee in a large pan. Add the poppy and mustard seeds and cook for 2 minutes, stirring.

Add the cayenne pepper, turmeric, garam masala, coriander, aubergine, red pepper, beans, tomatoes and

salt and pepper. Cover and cook for about 10 minutes.

Layer the rice and vegetable mixture in an ovenproof dish. Cover and cook in a preheated moderate oven (180 °C, 350 °F, Gas Mark 4) for 30 minutes.

Sprinkle with toasted pine nuts and raisins. Garnish with a coriander sprig and serve hot. **Serves 4**

Winter fruit salad

(Illustrated above)

75 g/3 oz (U.S. $\frac{1}{2}$ cup) dried prunes
75 g/3 oz (U.S. $\frac{1}{2}$ cup) dried apricots
300 ml/$\frac{1}{2}$ pint (U.S. $1\frac{1}{4}$ cups) cold water
1 banana, peeled and sliced
1 apple, cored and sliced
1 tablespoon lemon juice
1 tablespoon All Bran
1 orange, peeled, pith removed and segmented
1 tablespoon sesame seeds

Place the prunes, apricots and water in a bowl. Leave to soak overnight or for 6–8 hours.

Transfer to a pan, cover and cook until tender, about 20–30 minutes. Allow to cool.

Toss the banana and apple slices in the lemon juice and stir into the prune mixture with the All Bran and orange.

Mix well to blend then sprinkle with sesame seeds to serve. **Serves 2–3**

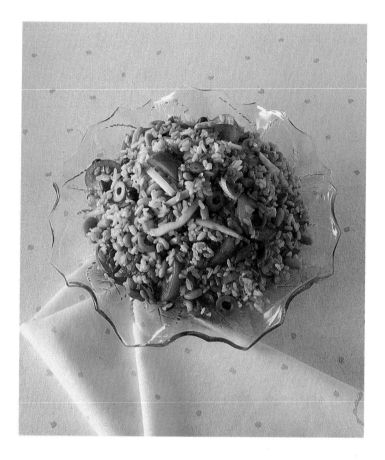

Tuscan bean and nut salad

(Illustrated above)

225 g/8 oz (u.s. generous 1 cup) long-grain brown
rice, cooked
1 green pepper, cored, seeded and sliced
1 yellow pepper, cored, seeded and sliced
4 tomatoes, cut into quarters
100 g/4 oz (u.s. $\frac{2}{3}$ cup) cooked flageolet, rose cocoa
or cannellini beans
50 g/2 oz (u.s. $\frac{1}{2}$ cup) hazelnuts, coarsely chopped
10 stuffed green olives, sliced
2 spring onions (u.s. scallions), trimmed and chopped
$\frac{1}{4}$ cucumber, cut into thin julienne strips
100 ml/4 fl oz (u.s. $\frac{1}{2}$ cup) French dressing

Place the rice, peppers, tomatoes, beans, hazelnuts, olives,
spring onions and cucumber in a bowl.

Pour over the dressing and toss to mix. Spoon into a
serving bowl and chill lightly; or spoon into an oiled
ring mould and turn out on to a plate to serve.

Serve with wedges of wholewheat bread. **Serves 4**

Mushroom and celery beanfeast

(Illustrated above)

3 tablespoons (u.s. 4 tablespoons) vegetable oil
1 teaspoon cumin seeds
2 small onions, peeled and chopped
2 stalks celery, scrubbed and sliced
1 garlic clove, peeled and crushed
1 × 398 g/14 oz can peeled tomatoes,
chopped
175 g/6 oz (u.s. 1$\frac{1}{2}$ cups) mushrooms, wiped
and sliced
$\frac{1}{2}$ teaspoon turmeric
$\frac{1}{2}$ teaspoon ground cumin
1 teaspoon coriander seeds
salt and freshly ground black pepper
450 g/1 lb cooked cannellini or blackeye beans
chopped fresh coriander to garnish

Heat the oil in a large pan. Add the cumin seeds and fry
for 1 minute. Stir in the onions, celery and garlic, blending well, and fry until softened, about 5 minutes.

Add the tomatoes, mushrooms, turmeric, cumin,
coriander seeds and salt and pepper to taste. Cook over
a gentle heat for 20 minutes.

Stir in the beans, blending well. Cover and cook for
a further 10 minutes.

Serve hot, sprinkled with chopped coriander. Serve
with wholewheat bread. **Serves 4**

Crunchy vegetable salad

(Illustrated opposite)

100 g/4 oz (U.S. $\frac{2}{3}$ cup) French beans, trimmed and
cut in half
100 g/4 oz (U.S. $\frac{2}{3}$ cup) carrots, peeled and cut into
thin julienne strips
100 g/4 oz shelled broad beans (U.S. $\frac{2}{3}$ cup fava or
lima beans)
100 g/4 oz (U.S. $\frac{2}{3}$ cup) raisins
Dressing
5 tablespoons (U.S. 6 tablespoons) olive oil
2 tablespoons wine vinegar
1 teaspoon Dijon mustard
$\frac{1}{2}$ teaspoon dried mixed herbs
salt and freshly ground black pepper

Cook the French beans and carrots in a pan of boiling
salted water for 5 minutes. Add the broad beans and
cook for a further 5 minutes. Drain and cool under cold
running water.

Mix the vegetables and raisins in a bowl, blending
well.

To make the dressing, place the oil, vinegar, mustard,
herbs and salt and pepper to taste in a screw-topped jar
and shake to mix.

Pour the dressing over the salad and toss gently to
mix. Serve lightly chilled. **Serves 4**

Chilli beansprouts

(Illustrated opposite)

225 g/8 oz (U.S. 4 cups) beansprouts, washed and
sorted
2 carrots, peeled and grated
50 g/2 oz (U.S. $\frac{1}{3}$ cup) raw peanuts
6 spring onions (U.S. scallions), trimmed and
chopped
100 g/4 oz (U.S. $\frac{2}{3}$ cup) raisins
Dressing
6 tablespoons (U.S. 7 tablespoons) sunflower oil
$\frac{1}{2}$ teaspoon chilli powder (U.S. chili powder)
1 teaspoon soy sauce
1 teaspoon clear honey
2 tablespoons lemon juice
salt and freshly ground black pepper

Mix the beansprouts with the carrots, peanuts, spring
onions and raisins, blending well.

To make the dressing, place the oil, chilli powder, soy
sauce, honey, lemon juice and salt and pepper to taste in
a screw-topped jar and shake to mix.

Pour the dressing over the salad and toss gently to
mix. Serve lightly chilled. **Serves 4**

Crunchy nut onions

4 large Spanish onions
50 g/2 oz (U.S. $\frac{1}{2}$ cup) cashew nuts
50 g/2 oz (U.S. $\frac{1}{2}$ cup) spicy-flavoured almonds
150 g/5 oz (U.S. 1 cup) long-grain rice, cooked
225 g/8 oz (U.S. 1 cup) tomatoes, peeled, seeded
and coarsely chopped
1 teaspoon curry powder
1 teaspoon turmeric
2–3 tablespoons (U.S. 3–4 tablespoons) sesame oil
salt and freshly ground black pepper

Do not peel the onions but boil in their skins in a pan of
salted water until tender, about 45 minutes. Allow to
cool.

Coarsely chop the nuts and mix with the rice,
tomatoes, curry powder, turmeric, oil and salt and
pepper to taste, blending well.

Using a sharp knife, cut away the root tip of each
onion but leave the coloured outer skin intact. Cut down
the length of each onion almost to the other side to
open out.

Divide the rice mixture between the onions to fill.
Place in a roasting tin. Cover and bake in a preheated
moderately hot oven (200°C, 400°F, Gas Mark 6) for
30–40 minutes. Serve hot. **Serves 4**

Above: Crunchy vegetable salad
Below: Chilli beansprouts

Raw food alternative

In an age when we constantly scrutinize the labels to cans, packets and food containers to find those seemingly-hidden extras like preservatives, sugar, flavour enhancers and stabilizers it is not perhaps surprising to learn that an ever-growing band of people are recommending the merits of eating food in its raw state.

Certainly food, if picked or harvested in its peak condition, should present itself at its best if taken this way – bursting with all the vitamins, minerals and other food nutrients that nature intended it will not need the processes of boiling, steaming, frying, baking and roasting or other nutrient-reducing cooking operations.

Followers justify a diet leaning almost exclusively to such foods on several levels: flavours are true and strong with such foods reducing the need for salt and other flavour enhancers; fibre level is likely to be high eliminating the need to take supplements for digestion; cooking failure is a thing of the past with such no-cook philosophy; speed is of the essence so here is a new kind of fast-food; and food values are high alongside food variety.

Such recommendations are convincing and I advocate a few 'raw' style dishes as part of a good balanced weekly vegetarian menu – and not just for the summer months when nature ensures its bounty of ripe fruit, vegetables, grains and nuts. In the winter, feast upon sprouted beans, winter root vegetables, tropical fruits and the vast selection of dairy produce.

Above: Beansprout and corn toss up *(recipe page 120)*
Right: Piquant pear salad *(recipe page 120)*
Below: Lunchtime avocados *(recipe page 120)*

Beansprout and corn toss up

(Illustrated on pages 118–119)

225 g/8 oz (U.S. 4 cups) beansprouts, washed
and sorted
100 g/4 oz (U.S. 1 cup) button mushrooms, wiped
8 radishes, trimmed and sliced
1 carrot, peeled and grated
1 × 335 g/11.8 oz can sweetcorn kernels (U.S. whole
kernel corn), drained
1 green pepper, cored, seeded and chopped
5 tablespoons (U.S. 6 tablespoons) French dressing
lettuce leaves

Place the beansprouts, mushrooms, radishes, carrot, sweet-corn and pepper in a bowl.

Pour over the dressing and toss gently to mix.

Line a serving plate with a few lettuce leaves. Pile the salad mixture on top and serve at once. **Serves 4**

Piquant pear salad

(Illustrated on pages 118–119)

½ onion, peeled and thinly sliced
1 red pepper, cored, seeded and sliced
1 green pepper, cored, seeded and sliced
350 g/12 oz (U.S. 2 cups) Red Leicester cheese, cubed
3 ripe Conference pears, cored and sliced
4 tomatoes, cut into wedges
8 black olives (U.S. ripe olives)
3–4 tablespoons French dressing
Chinese leaves

Place the onion, peppers, cheese, pears, tomatoes and olives in a bowl.

Pour over the dressing and toss gently to mix.

Line a serving plate with Chinese leaves (shredded if liked). Pile the salad mixture on top and serve at once. Serve with hot garlic bread if liked. **Serves 4**

Lunchtime avocados

(Illustrated on pages 118–119)

2 avocados
4 tablespoons (U.S. 5 tablespoons) oil
2 tablespoons cider vinegar
1 tablespoon chopped spring onion (U.S. scallion)
or red onion
2 teaspoons chopped fresh parsley or lemon balm
salt and freshly ground black pepper
175 g/6 oz (U.S. 1½ cups) Cheddar cheese or other
hard cheese, grated
spring onions (U.S. scallions) to garnish (optional)

Cut the avocados in half lengthwise. Remove and discard the stones (U.S. pits). Scoop out the flesh into bite-sized chunks and place in a bowl. Reserve the shells.

Mix the oil with the vinegar, spring onion or red onion, parsley or lemon balm and salt and pepper to taste, blending well.

Add to the avocado flesh with the cheese. Toss gently to mix.

Spoon the avocado mixture back into the avocado shells to serve. Serve with thin slices of wholewheat bread or bran crispbreads or crackers. **Serves 4**

Pear and ginger cartwheel

2 large ripe pears
2 tablespoons lemon juice
75 g/3 oz (U.S. 6 tablespoons) cream cheese
1–2 tablespoons mild curry mayonnaise or
dressing
2 pieces stem ginger in syrup, finely chopped
lettuce leaves
ground paprika to dust
mustard and cress to garnish

Peel, core and thinly slice the pears lengthways. Place in a bowl with the lemon juice and toss to coat.

Meanwhile, mix the cheese with the mayonnaise or dressing and ginger, blending well.

Line a serving plate with lettuce leaves and top with the pears, arranged in a cartwheel radiating from the centre of the plate. Pile the cheese mixture in the centre of the plate and dust with paprika.

Serve lightly chilled, garnished with mustard and cress. **Serves 2**

Dairy dip

Dairy dip

(Illustrated below)

300 ml/½ pint (U.S. 1¼ cups) soured cream
75 g/3 oz (U.S. ⅓ cup) cream cheese, softened
1 × 198 g/7 oz can sweetcorn kernels (U.S. whole kernel corn), drained
75 g/3 oz (U.S. ¾ cup) button mushrooms, wiped and finely sliced
2 teaspoons very finely chopped onion
¼ teaspoon mustard powder
3 drops Tabasco sauce (U.S. hot pepper sauce)
salt and freshly ground black pepper
raw vegetable crudités or crackers to serve
To garnish (optional)
lime slices
mint sprig

Mix the soured cream with the cream cheese, blending well.

Add the sweetcorn, mushrooms, onion, mustard powder, Tabasco sauce and salt and pepper to taste, blending well. Cover and chill for at least 4 hours or preferably overnight.

Serve with raw vegetable crudités or crackers as a light lunch or starter. **Serves 4–6**

Variations
Savoury apple dip Soften 225 g/8 oz (U.S. 1 cup) cream cheese with a hand-held mixer or food processor and gradually add 6 tablespoons (U.S. 7 tablespoons) apple juice to produce a smooth creamy mixture. Season to taste with celery salt and pepper. Transfer to a small serving bowl and sprinkle with 1 tablespoon chopped nuts.

Dairy apple and horseradish dip Mix 75 g/3 oz (U.S. ¾ cup) grated sweet apple with 2 tablespoons lemon juice. Add 8 tablespoons (U.S. 9 tablespoons) soured cream or mayonnaise and 1 tablespoon creamed horse-radish, blending well. Sprinkle with snipped chives to garnish.

Crunchy cheese and olive salad

(Illustrated above and on back cover)

50 g/2 oz (U.S. 1½ cups) Start cereal
50 g/2 oz (U.S. ⅓ cup) peanuts
100 g/4 oz (U.S. 1 cup) Gouda cheese, cut into thin strips
8 stoned (U.S. pitted) green olives, quartered
2 tomatoes, cut into wedges
2 tablespoons chopped fresh parsley
½ small crisp lettuce, shredded
French dressing (optional)

Place the cereal, peanuts, cheese, olives, tomatoes, parsley and lettuce in a salad bowl.

Add sufficient French dressing to moisten if liked, about 3–4 tablespoons. Toss gently to mix.

Serve at once with warm buttered wholewheat rolls.
Serves 4

Chèvre vinaigrette

(Illustrated above)

2 large oranges, peeled, pith removed and segmented
2 large pink or red grapefruit, peeled, pith removed and segmented
225 g/8 oz Buche de Chèvre or Montrachet cheese
Dressing
8 tablespoons (U.S. ½ cup) grapeseed oil
4 tablespoons (U.S. 5 tablespoons) white wine vinegar
2 teaspoons wholegrain mustard
1 egg yolk
salt and freshly ground black pepper
mint sprigs to garnish

Divide and attractively arrange the orange and grapefruit segments between four individual serving plates.

Slice the cheese using a wet knife and arrange over the fruit.

To make the dressing, beat the oil with the wine vinegar, mustard, egg yolk and salt and pepper to taste to make a thickened dressing.

Spoon the dressing over the fruit and cheese. Serve lightly chilled, garnished with sprigs of mint. **Serves 4**

Pitta salad pockets

(Illustrated above)

4 wholewheat pitta breads
175 g/6 oz (U.S. 2¼ cups) white cabbage, finely
shredded
2 carrots, peeled and grated
100 g/4 oz (U.S. ⅔ cup) raw peanuts, toasted
100 g/4 oz (U.S. ⅔ cup) raisins
25 g/1 oz (U.S. ¼ cup) sunflower seeds
2 tablespoons mayonnaise or salad cream
1 tablespoon oil
2 teaspoons vinegar
salt and freshly ground black pepper
parsley sprigs to garnish

Cut the pitta breads in half across the middle and open
out the pockets.

Mix the cabbage with the carrots, peanuts, raisins and
sunflower seeds.

Blend the mayonnaise or salad cream with the oil,
vinegar and salt and pepper to taste. Add to the vegetable
mixture and toss well to coat.

Stuff the pitta breads with the salad mixture and
garnish with parsley sprigs. **Makes 8**

Blue cheese dip

(Illustrated above)

100 g/4 oz Danish Blue cheese
2 tablespoons mayonnaise
150 ml/¼ pint (U.S. ⅔ cup) whipping cream
freshly ground black pepper
cucumber slices
parsley sprig to garnish
To serve
vegetable crudités
savoury biscuits (U.S. savory crackers)

Mash the blue cheese until smooth. Beat in the mayonnaise, blending well.

Whip the cream until it stands in soft peaks. Fold into
the cheese mixture with pepper to taste.

Line a small serving bowl with cucumber slices. Pile
the dip on top and garnish with a cucumber slice and
parsley sprig. Serve lightly chilled with vegetable crudités
and savoury biscuits (U.S. savory crackers). **Serves 4**

Variations
Blue cheese and pepper dip Prepare as above but
add ½ cored, seeded and chopped green pepper with the
cream.
Blue cheese and walnut dip Prepare as above but
add 25–50 g/1–2 oz (U.S. ¼–½ cup) finely chopped
walnuts with the cream.

Fruit and nut slaw

(Illustrated left)

225 g/8 oz (U.S. 3 cups) white cabbage, shredded
1 large carrot, peeled and grated or cut into julienne strips
2 stalks celery, scrubbed and sliced
6 spring onions (U.S. scallions), trimmed and chopped
1 × 335 g/11.8 oz can sweetcorn kernels (U.S. whole kernel corn), drained
2 red eating apples, cored and chopped
2 teaspoons lemon juice
100 g/4 oz (U.S. 1 cup) walnut halves, coarsely chopped
100 g/4 oz (U.S. $\frac{2}{3}$ cup) fresh dates, stoned and chopped
Dressing
5 tablespoons (U.S. $\frac{1}{3}$ cup) vegetable oil
2–3 tablespoons orange juice
1 tablespoon bran
salt and freshly ground black pepper

Toss the cabbage with the carrot, celery, spring onions and sweetcorn kernels.

Toss the apples in the lemon juice and add to the cabbage mixture with the walnuts and dates, blending well.

To make the dressing, mix the oil with the orange juice, bran and salt and pepper to taste, blending well.

Pour over the salad and toss gently to mix. Serve at once. **Serves 4–6**

Niblets cocktail

(Illustrated below)

1 × 198 g/7 oz can sweetcorn kernels (U.S. whole
kernel corn), drained
1 teaspoon grated onion
1 tablespoon mayonnaise
salt and freshly ground black pepper
shredded lettuce
watercress sprigs
cayenne pepper

Mix the sweetcorn kernels with the onion, mayonnaise
and salt and pepper to taste, blending well.

Arrange a little shredded lettuce and watercress sprigs
in four serving glasses. Spoon the corn mixture on top
and sprinkle with cayenne pepper.

Serve lightly chilled with brown bread and butter.
Serves 4

Avocado and corn salad

(Illustrated below)

1 × 198 g/7 oz can sweetcorn kernels (U.S. whole
kernel corn), drained
75 g/3 oz (U.S. $\frac{3}{4}$ cup) button mushrooms, wiped
and sliced
$\frac{1}{4}$ cucumber, chopped
2 avocados, peeled, stoned and sliced
4 tablespoons (U.S. 5 tablespoons) olive oil
2 tablespoons white wine or cider vinegar
salt and freshly ground black pepper
25 g/1 oz flaked almonds (U.S. $\frac{1}{4}$ cup slivered almonds),
toasted

Mix the sweetcorn kernels with the mushrooms, cucumber and avocados.

Whisk the oil with the vinegar and salt and pepper to
taste.

Pour over the salad and toss gently to mix. Spoon
into a serving dish and sprinkle with the almonds to
serve. **Serves 4**

Left: *Fruit and nut slaw*
Centre: *Niblets cocktail*
Right: *Avocado and corn salad*

Storecupboard standbys

With a little careful thought, subtle and clever blending of imaginative ingredients and a well-stocked storecupboard, you will see in this chapter just how easy it is to produce a memorable meal at a moment's notice. Whether you have forgotten to go to the shops, need to feed an unexpected crowd at short notice or simply over-extended your budget and need to rely upon what is available, the choices can be as varied as Mixed Bean Casserole, Bruzzoni Macaroni or Egg and Corn Fricassée.

Organization is the keyword to this section, for undoubtedly a few well stored cans of produce, a good selection of versatile chilled refrigerator items and a freezer with a few standbys will save the day. Mixed and matched with a few cook's indispensable aids like dried herbs, spices and other seasonings you'll have the makings of an excellent meal.

Good storecupboard items include dried peas, beans and lentils, pasta in all its shapes and guises, dried fruit and nuts, a comprehensive selection of cereals and grains, dried vegetables and soups as well as the odd packet of quick-mix bread. Canned items of value include some vegetables like sweetcorn, tomatoes and mushrooms and fruits like apricots which have a short fresh season and can well. A good chilled refrigerator 'storecupboard' will invariably include milk, eggs, yogurt and cheese, not forgetting fruit juices and perhaps some ready-made pastry.

A ready-prepared freezer meal will be a bonus but a few special 'bulk' extras and anchors are likely to prove more versatile – included in these come plain pancakes, baked pastry cases ready for filling and a few made-up sauces for pasta and rice as well as bread items.

Above left: *Egg and corn fricassée (recipe page 128)*
Above right: *Popeye's savoury puff (recipe page 128)*
Below: *Bruzzoni macaroni (recipe page 132)*

Egg and corn fricassée

(Illustrated on pages 126–127)

6 eggs
50 g/2 oz (U.S. $\frac{1}{4}$ cup) butter
3 tablespoons (U.S. 4 tablespoons) flour
300 ml/$\frac{1}{2}$ pint (U.S. 1$\frac{1}{4}$ cups) milk
300 ml/$\frac{1}{2}$ pint (U.S. 1$\frac{1}{4}$ cups) vegetable stock or water
1 × 340 g/12 oz can sweetcorn kernels (U.S. whole kernel corn), drained
6 tablespoons (U.S. 7 tablespoons) cooked peas
salt and freshly ground black pepper
chopped fresh parsley to garnish
triangles of hot toast to serve

Place the eggs in a pan of cold water. Bring to the boil and cook for 4 minutes. Drain and rinse in cold water. Carefully remove the shells, then keep the eggs hot in a bowl of warm water.

Melt the butter in a pan. Stir in the flour and cook for 1 minute. Mix the milk with the stock or water. Remove the pan from the heat and gradually add the milk and stock to the flour mixture, blending well. Bring to the boil and cook for 2–3 minutes, stirring constantly, until smooth and thickened.

Add the sweetcorn, peas, whole soft-boiled eggs and salt and pepper to taste, blending well. Simmer gently for 2–3 minutes.

Spoon into a warmed serving dish and sprinkle with chopped parsley. Serve at once with triangles of hot toast. **Serves 4**

Popeye's savoury puff

(Illustrated on pages 126–127)

Choux pastry
150 g/5 oz plain flour (U.S. 1$\frac{1}{4}$ cups all-purpose flour)
pinch of salt
100 g/4 oz (U.S. $\frac{1}{2}$ cup) butter or margarine
300 ml/$\frac{1}{2}$ pint (U.S. 1$\frac{1}{4}$ cups) water
4 eggs, beaten
Filling
25 g/1 oz (U.S. 2 tablespoons) butter
1 × 200 g/8 oz packet frozen chopped or leaf spinach
50 g/2 oz plain flour (U.S. $\frac{1}{2}$ cup all-purpose flour)
450 ml/$\frac{3}{4}$ pint (U.S. 2 cups) milk
100 g/4 oz (U.S. 1 cup) Cheddar cheese, grated
225 g/8 oz (U.S. 2 cups) cooked mushrooms
salt and freshly ground black pepper

To make the pastry, sift together the flour and salt. Place the butter or margarine and water in a pan and slowly bring to the boil. Remove from the heat and stir in the flour, blending well. Beat until the paste is smooth and forms a ball in the pan. Allow to cool slightly then beat in the eggs, a little at a time. The mixture should be smooth, glossy and of a piping consistency.

To make the filling, melt the butter in a pan. Add the spinach and cook over a low heat until the spinach is completely thawed. Stir in the flour, blending well. Gradually add the milk and cook until the mixture thickens. Add the cheese and stir until melted. Add the mushrooms and salt and pepper to taste, blending well.

Spoon the choux paste into a piping bag (U.S. pastry bag) fitted with a 1 cm/$\frac{1}{2}$ inch star nozzle. Pipe choux paste around the edge of a 5 cm/2 inch deep 1.2 litre/2 pint (U.S. 5 cup) buttered ovenproof dish. Pour the filling carefully into the centre.

Bake in a preheated moderately hot oven (200°C, 400°F, Gas Mark 6) for 30–40 minutes until the pastry is well risen and golden brown. Serve at once. **Serves 4**

Vegetable and cheesy yogurt lasagne

3 tablespoons (U.S. 4 tablespoons) oil
450 g/1 lb mixed prepared vegetables (e.g. leeks, peppers, mushrooms, celery, tomatoes and onion)
pinch of mixed dried herbs
300 ml/$\frac{1}{2}$ pint (U.S. 1$\frac{1}{4}$ cups) vegetable stock
4 tablespoons spring onion flavoured dressing
(U.S. 5 tablespoons scallion flavored dressing)
or mayonnaise
salt and freshly ground black pepper
175 g/6 oz lasagne verdi
150 ml/$\frac{1}{4}$ pint (U.S. $\frac{2}{3}$ cup) natural yogurt
75 g/3 oz (U.S. $\frac{3}{4}$ cup) Cheddar cheese, grated

Heat the oil in a pan. Add the vegetables and herbs and fry for 5 minutes. Add the stock, blending well, and cook for a further 10 minutes or until the vegetables begin to soften.

Stir in half of the spring onion dressing and salt and pepper to taste, blending well. Layer the vegetable mixture and pasta in an ovenproof dish, finishing with a layer of lasagne.

Mix the yogurt with the cheese, remaining dressing and salt and pepper to taste, blending well. Spoon over the lasagne. Cook in a preheated moderate oven (180°C, 350°F, Gas Mark 4) for 40–50 minutes or until tender and golden. **Serves 4**

Devilled mushrooms

Devilled mushrooms

(Illustrated below)

25 g/1 oz (U.S. 2 tablespoons) butter
175 g/6 oz (U.S. 1½ cups) mushrooms, wiped and
sliced
1 tablespoon flour
150 ml/¼ pint (U.S. ⅔ cup) milk
2 teaspoons Worcestershire sauce
1 teaspoon French mustard
1 tablespoon tomato purée
4 slices hot buttered wholewheat toast
chopped fresh parsley to garnish

Melt the butter in a pan. Add the mushrooms and sauté for 2 minutes.

Stir in the flour and cook for 1 minute. Gradually add the milk, Worcestershire sauce, mustard and tomato purée, blending well. Bring to the boil, stirring constantly, reduce the heat and simmer for 2 minutes.

Spoon on to the toast and sprinkle with chopped parsley. Cut into triangles to serve. **Serves 4**

Wholewheat pittas

1 tablespoon oil
50 g/2 oz (U.S. ¼ cup) butter or margarine
1 aubergine (U.S. eggplant), cut into 1 cm/½ inch cubes
100 g/4 oz (U.S. 1 cup) mushrooms, wiped
and sliced
1 onion, peeled and sliced
2 tomatoes, chopped
1 × 335 g/11½ oz can sweetcorn kernels (U.S. whole
kernel corn), drained
½ teaspoon chilli powder
1 teaspoon chopped fresh parsley
2 tablespoons tomato purée
salt and freshly ground black pepper
4 large wholewheat pitta breads, split and warmed

Heat the oil and butter or margarine until hot. Add the aubergine cubes and fry until golden, about 5 minutes.

Stir in the mushrooms and onion and cook for a further 5 minutes. Add the tomatoes, corn, chilli powder, parsley, tomato purée and salt and pepper to taste, blending well. Simmer gently for 10 minutes.

Divide the mixture evenly between the split warmed pitta breads and serve at once in napkins. **Serves 4**

Mixed bean casserole

75 g/3 oz (U.S. 6 tablespoons) butter
1 large onion, peeled and thinly sliced
1 garlic clove, peeled and crushed
100 g/4 oz (U.S. 1 cup) French beans, trimmed
3 courgettes (U.S. zucchini), thickly sliced
100 g/4 oz (U.S. 1 cup) button mushrooms, wiped
200 ml/7 fl oz (U.S. $\frac{7}{8}$ cup) vegetable stock
salt and freshly ground black pepper
2 bay leaves
fresh thyme or rosemary sprig
2 × 450 g/1 lb cans barbecue beans
1 × 335 g/12 oz can sweetcorn kernels (U.S. whole
kernel corn), drained
4–5 tablespoons canned chick garbanzo peas
8 small slices wholewheat French bread
100 g/4 oz (U.S. 1 cup) cheese, grated

Melt 25 g/1 oz (U.S. 2 tablespoons) of the butter in a pan. Add the onion and garlic and cook for 4–5 minutes.

Transfer to a casserole and add the French beans, courgettes, mushrooms, stock, salt and pepper, bay leaves and thyme or rosemary. Cover and cook in a moderate oven (180°C, 350°F, Gas Mark 4) for 25 minutes.

Remove from the oven and stir in the barbecue beans, sweetcorn and chick peas, blending well. Cover, return to the oven and cook for a further 20 minutes.

Toast both sides of the bread slices. Spread one side with butter and sprinkle with the cheese. Grill until golden. Serve casserole topped with croûtes. **Serves 4**

Hot cheese stuffed eggs

(Illustrated above)

4 hard-boiled eggs (U.S. hard-cooked eggs), shelled
50 g/2 oz (U.S. $\frac{1}{4}$ cup) butter, softened
75 g/3 oz (U.S. $\frac{3}{4}$ cup) Cheddar cheese, grated
1 garlic clove, peeled and crushed (optional)
1 tablespoon cream or top of the milk (U.S. half
and half)
salt and cayenne pepper
1 recipe hot Cheese sauce (see page 84)
To garnish
cooked mushrooms
watercress sprigs

Halve the eggs lengthwise, remove the yolks and place in a bowl. Add the butter, 50 g/2 oz (U.S. $\frac{1}{2}$ cup) of the cheese, garlic if used, cream and salt and cayenne pepper to taste. Mash until smooth.

Spoon the mixture back into the egg whites. Place the stuffed eggs in a greased flameproof dish.

Spoon over the hot cheese sauce and sprinkle with the remaining cheese. Cook under a preheated hot grill (U.S. broiler) until golden and bubbly. Serve hot, garnished with cooked mushrooms and watercress sprigs. **Serves 4**

Cheese loaf

(Illustrated above)

175 g/6 oz (U.S. scant 1 cup) long-grain rice, cooked
75 g/3 oz (U.S. ¾ cup) Mozzarella cheese, grated
75 g/3 oz (U.S. ¾ cup) Lancashire cheese, grated
1 egg, beaten
225 ml/7½ fl oz (U.S. scant 1 cup) milk
1 teaspoon dried mixed herbs
To garnish
red pepper rings
green pepper rings
lettuce leaves

Mix the rice with the cheeses, egg, milk and herbs, blending well.

Spoon the mixture into a greased 450 g/1 lb loaf tin. Bake in a preheated moderately hot oven (190°C, 375°F, Gas Mark 5) for 15–20 minutes or until firm to the touch.

Turn out on to a serving plate and serve hot or cold, garnished with red and green pepper rings and lettuce. **Serves 4**

Savoury tamale bake

50 g/2 oz chicken flavour textured soya vegetable protein
100 ml/4 fl oz (U.S. ½ cup) hot water
2 tablespoons oil
1 onion, peeled and chopped
1 green pepper, cored, seeded and chopped
1 × 425 g/15 oz can chilli beans (U.S. chili beans)
2 tomatoes, skinned and chopped
salt and freshly ground black pepper
Topping
100 g/4 oz (U.S. ¾ cup) yellow cornmeal
1½ teaspoons baking powder
½ teaspoon salt
1 egg, beaten
100 ml/4 fl oz (U.S. ½ cup) milk
1 tablespoon melted butter
25 g/1 oz (U.S. ¼ cup) Cheddar cheese, grated

Place the textured soya vegetable protein in a bowl with the hot water. Leave for 3–4 minutes to rehydrate.

Heat the oil in a pan. Add the onion and green pepper and fry until softened, about 5 minutes. Add the textured soya vegetable protein, chilli beans, tomatoes and salt and pepper to taste, blending well. Bring to the boil, stirring occasionally. Spoon into an ovenproof dish.

Mix the cornmeal with the baking powder and salt. Gradually add the egg, milk and butter to make a smooth mixture. Pour over the bean mixture and sprinkle with the cheese. Cook in a preheated moderately hot oven (200°C, 400°F, Gas Mark 6) for 20 minutes until the topping is set and golden. Serve at once. **Serves 4**

Bruzzoni macaroni

(Illustrated below and on pages 126–127)

175 g/6 oz (u.s. 1½ cups) wholewheat macaroni
600 ml/1 pint (u.s. 2½ cups) white sauce (see page 84)
100 g/4 oz (u.s. 1 cup) Cheddar cheese, grated
225 g/8 oz (u.s. 1 cup) frozen leaf spinach, thawed
and coarsely chopped
1 × 335 g/11.8 oz can sweetcorn kernels (u.s. whole
kernel corn), drained
50 g/2 oz (u.s. ¼ cup) cottage cheese
½ teaspoon grated nutmeg
salt and freshly ground black pepper
5 tablespoons (u.s. 6 tablespoons) wholewheat
breadcrumbs
To garnish
tomato slices
parsley sprig

Cook the macaroni in a pan of boiling salted water until tender, according to the packet instructions. Drain thoroughly and mix with half of the sauce and the cheese, blending well.

Mix the spinach with the remaining sauce, sweetcorn and cottage cheese. Stir in the nutmeg and salt and pepper to taste.

Place the spinach and corn mixture on the base of an ovenproof dish. Cover with the macaroni cheese and sprinkle with the breadcrumbs.

Bake in a preheated moderately hot oven (200 °C, 400 °F, Gas Mark 6) for 30 minutes or until golden and bubbly. Garnish and serve hot. **Serves 4**

Beaumont goulash

(Illustrated below)

3 tablespoons (u.s. 4 tablespoons) oil
1 onion, peeled and sliced
2 garlic cloves, peeled and crushed
3 stalks celery, scrubbed and sliced
1 tablespoon paprika
1 tablespoon caraway seeds
2 tablespoons tomato purée
150 ml/¼ pint (u.s. ⅔ cup) vegetable stock
1 × 398 g/14 oz can peeled tomatoes
1 × 335 g/11.8 oz can sweetcorn kernels (u.s. whole
kernel corn), drained
2 tablespoons chopped fresh parsley
1 × 398 g/14 oz can cannellini beans, drained
salt and freshly ground black pepper
150 ml/¼ pint (u.s. ⅔ cup) soured cream
chopped fresh parsley to garnish

Heat the oil in a pan. Add the onion, garlic and celery and sauté until softened, about 5 minutes. Add the paprika and caraway seeds and cook for 1 minute.

Stir in the tomato purée, vegetable stock and tomatoes, blending well. Bring to the boil, reduce the heat and simmer for 30 minutes.

Mix in the sweetcorn kernels, parsley, cannellini beans and salt and pepper to taste. Cook over a gentle heat for 15 minutes.

Remove from the heat and place in a warmed serving dish. Swirl with the soured cream and sprinkle with chopped parsley. Serve with brown rice or wholewheat rolls. **Serves 4**

Left: *Bruzzoni macaroni*
Below: *Beaumont goulash*

Slimmers' vegetarian dishes

Vegetarians, like meat-eaters, are not excluded from and share the agonies of weight-reducing or weight control just like other groups who practise a special diet. They do however have luck on their side, for by their nature, vegetarian associated foods like fruits, vegetables, beans and their sprouts are generally low in calories but high in nutrients. There are few fat-laden items like red meats, game and poultry to contend with. Weighed against more calorie-rich foods like some dairy produce, nuts and cereals there is the perfect repertoire of foods for a good calorie-reducing vegetarian diet that is full of variety, high on sustenance and restrictive only to a minor degree.

For simplicity most slimmers opt for a calorie-reducing diet to practise weight control – it fits in neatly with social arrangements, is flexible for eating away from home and is measurable to a high degree. The recipes in this section have therefore been calorie counted to the nearest 5 calorie units. Portion sizes may be smaller than you are traditionally used to – but this is a diet after all!

For success, plan a day's or week's eating pattern well ahead and steer clear of the kitchen with its temptations until meal time – or ensure that you have a full stomach. The same applies when shopping – don't be tempted to buy a constantly-tempting item because of a few tummy rumbles and put back your goal.

However remember diets are for healthy people (check with your doctor if in doubt) and take the pace slowly but steadily – few crash diets work in the long term if they do not fit in with a good balanced and appetizing long-term eating pattern.

Above left: *Red bean bake (recipe page 136)*
Above right: *Potato salad (recipe page 138)*
Centre: *Pineapple pepper risotto (recipe page 136)*
Below left: *Special fruit salad (recipe page 138)*
Below right: *Crunchy coleslaw (recipe page 138)*

Pineapple pepper risotto

(Illustrated on pages 134–135)

2 teaspoons reduced fat spread
2 tablespoons chopped onion
175 g/6 oz (U.S. scant 1 cup) long-grain rice
1 can low calorie spring vegetable soup
150 ml/¼ pint (U.S. ⅔ cup) unsweetened pineapple juice
150 ml/¼ pint (U.S. ⅔ cup) water
1 medium green pepper, cored, seeded and sliced
100 g/4 oz (U.S. ¾ cup) unsweetened canned pineapple
pieces, drained
salt and freshly ground black pepper
50 g/2 oz (U.S. ½ cup) Cheddar cheese, grated
2 tablespoons chopped fresh parsley (optional)

Melt the spread in a saucepan or flameproof casserole. Add the onion and cook gently until beginning to soften. Mix in the rice and continue to cook for 3–4 minutes, stirring constantly.

Add the soup, pineapple juice, water and green pepper, blending well. Bring to the boil, stir well, cover, reduce the heat and simmer very gently until the rice is cooked and all the liquid has been absorbed, about 15–20 minutes.

Stir in the pineapple pieces and salt and pepper to taste, blending well. Heat through until hot.

To serve, divide the risotto between four serving plates. Top each with a quarter of the grated cheese. Sprinkle with parsley and serve at once.
Serves 4   Calories per serving 293

Red bean bake

(Illustrated on pages 134–135)

1 can low calorie spring vegetable soup
350 g/12 oz (U.S. 2 cups) canned cooked red kidney beans
½ teaspoon mustard powder
2 teaspoons white wine
1 bay leaf
pepper
8 teaspoons dry breadcrumbs
pinch of dried thyme or marjoram
2 tablespoons chopped fresh herbs (e.g. chives and
parsley) (optional)

Heat the soup in a pan until hot, then mix with the beans, blending well.

Stir in the mustard, wine, bay leaf and pepper to taste, blending well. Spoon into a flameproof casserole. Bake, uncovered, in a preheated moderate oven (160°C, 325°F, Gas Mark 3) for 45 minutes.

Mix the breadcrumbs with the dried herbs and sprinkle evenly over the beans. Cook under a preheated hot grill (U.S. broiler) until crisp and golden. Sprinkle with fresh herbs. **Serves 4   Calories per serving 133**

Mushrooms à la grecque

4 tablespoons (U.S. 5 tablespoons) oil
1 large garlic clove, peeled and crushed
2 onions, peeled and chopped
400 ml/14 fl oz (U.S. 1¾ cups) dry white wine
8 tablespoons (U.S. 9 tablespoons) tomato purée
2 teaspoons dried mixed herbs
8 tomatoes, peeled, seeded and chopped
675 g/1½ lb button mushrooms, wiped
chopped fresh parsley to garnish
4 × 50 g/2 oz wholewheat bread rolls to serve

Place the oil, garlic and onion in a pan and cook for 4–5 minutes to soften. Add the wine, tomato purée, herbs and tomatoes. Simmer, uncovered, for 5 minutes.

Add the mushrooms and cook for a further 3–4 minutes, stirring occasionally. Allow to cool and chill lightly.

Serve cold, sprinkled with chopped parsley. Serve with the wholewheat rolls for a light lunch or supper dish.
Serves 4   Calories per serving 390 (including roll)

Quick wholewheat pizza

136

Quick wholewheat pizza

(Illustrated above)

4 × 50 g/2 oz soft round wholewheat rolls
1 garlic clove, peeled and crushed
½ teaspoon salt
4 teaspoons reduced fat spread
4 teaspoons tomato purée
8 slices reduced fat processed cheese
½ teaspoon dried thyme
8 anchovy fillets
8 stuffed olives, sliced
basil sprig to garnish (optional)

Cut each roll in half. Mix the garlic with the salt and spread, blending well. Spread over the cut surfaces of the rolls. Toast under a preheated hot grill (U.S. broiler) until lightly browned.

Spread with the tomato purée and top each with a slice of cheese. Sprinkle with the thyme and garnish with an anchovy fillet and stuffed olive slices.

Return to the grill and cook until hot and bubbly, about 5 minutes. Serve hot.

Serves 4   Calories per serving 291

Caesar salad

4 slices wholewheat bread
50 g/2 oz (U.S. ¼ cup) low-fat spread
100 g/4 oz (U.S. 2 cups) lettuce, shredded
350 g/12 oz (U.S. 3 cups) cucumber, diced
4 tomatoes, sliced
4 hard-boiled eggs (U.S. hard-cooked), shelled and quartered
4 tablespoons (U.S. 5 tablespoons) low-fat mayonnaise
50 g/2 oz (U.S. ½ cup) Cheddar cheese, grated

Cut the bread into small neat dice. Melt the low-fat spread in a non-stick frying pan (U.S. skillet). Add the bread cubes and toss gently, taking care to keep the cubes separate. Cook slowly until crisp then drain on absorbent kitchen paper.

Place the lettuce, cucumber, tomatoes and egg in a serving bowl and toss gently together. Top with the mayonnaise and grated cheese. Scatter the croûtons over the salad to serve. **Serves 4   Calories per serving 350**

Potato salad

(Illustrated on pages 134–135)

350 g/12 oz potatoes, cooked in their skins
2 teaspoons wine vinegar
8 teaspoons reduced calorie dressing
1 small onion, peeled and thinly sliced
2 teaspoons drained capers
2 tablespoons chopped fresh parsley

Peel the potatoes while still warm, slice into a bowl and sprinkle with the vinegar.

Spoon over the dressing and toss gently to mix.

Add the onion slices and capers, blending gently. Sprinkle with parsley and serve cold but not chilled.
Serves 4   Calories per serving 97

Crunchy coleslaw

(Illustrated on pages 134–135)

4 tablespoons (U.S. 5 tablespoons) reduced calorie dressing
4 tablespoons (U.S. 5 tablespoons) low-fat natural yogurt
squeeze of lemon juice
$\frac{1}{2}$ teaspoon paprika
salt
175 g/6 oz (U.S. $2\frac{1}{4}$ cups) white cabbage, shredded
75 g/3 oz (U.S. $\frac{3}{4}$ cup) carrots, peeled and coarsely grated
75 g/3 oz (U.S. $\frac{3}{4}$ cup) celery, scrubbed and chopped
1 apple, cored and chopped
1 onion, peeled and thinly sliced
2–3 tablespoons chopped fresh parsley

Mix the dressing with the yogurt, blending well. Add the lemon juice, paprika and salt to taste, mixing well to blend.

Stir in the cabbage, carrots, celery and apple. Transfer to a serving bowl.

Top with the sliced onion and parsley.
Serves 4   Calories per serving 69

Special fruit salad

(Illustrated on pages 134–135)

$\frac{1}{2}$ ripe honeydew melon
1 medium banana
1 tablespoon lemon juice
150 g/5 oz (U.S. 1 cup) strawberries
100 g/4 oz (U.S. 1 cup) canned peach slices in natural fruit juice
4 teaspoons reduced sugar strawberry jam

Peel, then cut the melon flesh into chunks. Peel and slice the banana and toss in the lemon juice. Hull, then halve or slice the strawberries, reserving four small berries for the decoration.

Drain the juice from the peaches and reserve 4 tablespoons (U.S. 5 tablespoons). Place all the fruits in a bowl. Mix the reserved peach juice with the strawberry jam, blending well. Stir gently into the fruit salad. Cover and chill lightly.

To serve, divide the fruit salad evenly between four dessert glasses and top each with a reserved whole strawberry. **Serves 4   Calories per serving 79**

Egg and watercress mousses

1 small bunch watercress, trimmed
2 hard-boiled (U.S. hard-cooked) eggs, shelled and very finely chopped
4 tablespoons (U.S. 5 tablespoons) low-calorie or low-fat mayonnaise
3 tablespoons (U.S. 4 tablespoons) natural yogurt
1 teaspoon powdered gelatine
1 teaspoon lemon juice
2 teaspoons water
salt and freshly ground black pepper
1 small egg white
4 bran crispbreads to serve

Reserve a few watercress sprigs for the garnish and finely chop the remainder. Mix the chopped watercress with the hard-boiled eggs, mayonnaise and yogurt.

Dissolve the gelatine in the lemon juice and water and fold into the watercress mixture with salt and pepper to taste.

Whisk the egg white until it stands in stiff peaks and fold into the mixture. Turn into two small dishes or moulds and chill to set.

Garnish with the reserved watercress sprigs and serve each mousse with two crispbreads.
Serves 2   Calories per serving 250 (including crispbreads)

Tomato sauce

Tomato sauce

(Illustrated below)

1 onion, peeled and chopped
2 garlic cloves, peeled and crushed
2 teaspoons reduced fat spread
1 can low calorie tomato soup
1 bay leaf
pinch of dried thyme or marjoram
2 tablespoons lemon juice
1 tablespoon chopped fresh herbs (e.g. basil, chives and parsley)
salt and freshly ground black pepper

Place the onion, garlic and spread in a pan. Heat gently and cook until softened, about 5 minutes.

Add the soup, bay leaf and dried herbs, blending well. Bring to the boil, reduce the heat and simmer gently for 15 minutes.

Remove and discard the bay leaf. Stir in the lemon juice, fresh herbs and salt and pepper to taste. Serve hot with pasta or hard-boiled eggs.

Serves 4   Calories per serving 34

Crunchy melon salad

350 g/12 oz (U.S. ¾ lb) honeydew melon, cubed
50 g/2 oz (U.S. ½ cup) walnuts, coarsely broken
50 g/2 oz (U.S. ⅓ cup) raisins
4 teaspoons finely chopped onion
Dressing
4 tablespoons (U.S. 5 tablespoons) oil-free French dressing
4 tablespoons (U.S. 5 tablespoons) natural yogurt
2 tablespoons chopped fresh parsley
dash of French mustard
lettuce or Chinese leaves to serve

Mix the melon with the walnuts, raisins and onion, blending well.

To make the dressing, mix the oil-free French dressing with the yogurt, parsley and mustard to taste. Pour over the melon mixture and toss to coat.

Line four small dishes with shredded lettuce or Chinese leaves and spoon over the melon salad. Serve at once.
Serves 4   Calories per serving 155

Grilled peaches with raspberry sauce

(Illustrated above)

4 teaspoons reduced fat spread
4 wholemeal digestive biscuits (U.S. wholewheat
graham crackers), crushed
$\frac{1}{4}$ teaspoon almond essence (U.S. almond extract)
8 canned peach halves in fruit juice, drained with
8 tablespoons (U.S. $\frac{1}{2}$ cup) juice reserved
8 teaspoons reduced sugar raspberry jam
8 tablespoons (U.S. $\frac{1}{2}$ cup) low-fat natural yogurt

Melt the spread in a pan. Add the biscuit crumbs and almond essence and stir to coat.

Spoon an equal amount of the crumb mixture into the cavity of each peach half, reserving the remaining crumb mixture. Place in a flameproof dish.

Cook the peaches under a preheated moderate grill (U.S. broiler) for 3–4 minutes. Arrange in small serving dishes.

Warm the reserved juice in a pan with the jam, blending well. Pour half over the peaches and sprinkle with the remaining crumb mixture.

Spoon 2 tablespoons of the yogurt around each portion before serving, swirl in the remaining jam mixture. Serve at once. **Serves 4   Calories per serving 183**

Variations

Grilled apricots with raspberry sauce Prepare and cook as before but use 12 canned apricot halves in fruit juice instead of the peach halves. Serve three apricot halves per portion.

Grilled pears with raspberry sauce Prepare and cook as before but use 8 canned pear halves in fruit juice instead of the peach halves.

Grilled peaches with strawberry sauce Prepare and cook as before but use reduced sugar strawberry jam instead of the raspberry jam for the sauce.

Baked sponge puddings

(Illustrated above)

4 tablespoons (U.S. 5 tablespoons) reduced fat spread
4 teaspoons castor sugar (U.S. superfine sugar)
135 g/4½ oz self-raising flour (U.S. 1 cup plus
2 tablespoons self-rising flour sifted
with 1 teaspoon baking powder)
2 eggs
1 teaspoon vegetable oil
4 teaspoons reduced sugar strawberry jam

Cream the spread with the sugar until light and fluffy. Sprinkle in a little flour and beat in the eggs, one at a time, blending well. Fold in the remaining flour.

Spoon the mixture into four oiled non-stick individual baking tins. Bake in a preheated moderate oven (180°C, 350°F, Gas Mark 4) for 15 minutes. Allow to cool slightly, then turn out to serve.

Warm the jam gently and spoon over the sponge puddings. Serve at once.
Serves 4   Calories per serving 270

Fruity baked apples

4 × 225 g/8 oz cooking apples (U.S. 4 × ½ lb tart apples)
50 g/2 oz (U.S. ⅓ cup) stoneless dates, chopped
25 g/1 oz (U.S. 3 tablespoons) raisins
4 teaspoons brown sugar
pinch of ground cinnamon
8 tablespoons (U.S. 9 tablespoons) apple juice
or water

Wash the apples and remove the cores. Make a shallow cut around the middle of each apple to prevent bursting during cooking.

Mix the dates with the raisins, sugar and cinnamon and use to fill the apple cavities, pressing down firmly. Place in an ovenproof dish and pour the apple juice or water around the apples.

Cover and bake in a moderate oven (180°C, 350°F, Gas Mark 4) for about 40 minutes or until tender but not fallen. Serve hot or cold with a little natural yogurt if liked. **Serves 4   Calories per serving 135**

Puddings and desserts

Crisp, flaky and fruity; iced, creamy and mouth-watering; or bubbling hot, soothing and indulgently sweet – there is the perfect pudding to round off any delicious vegetarian meal: The choice is wide and varied and will suit all pockets from the pauper's to the princely; all seasons from the light summer appetite to the stomach-warming winter one; and all occasions from the simple mid-week supper to the grand and sumptuous celebration dinner.

It is often said that if the appetizer teases the palate then the pudding or dessert should tempt it – after a pleasing starter and a hearty main course then appetites start to wane and so need re-awakening. If in doubt about what to choose then fall back on the reassuring hand of mother nature and follow the seasons. Each season will bring its peak ripe crop of fresh fruits and nuts to lend a hand with culinary inspiration.

In the spring consider the best of citrus fruits alongside plain cooked early forced rhubarb in dishes like Scotch Pancakes with Lemon Butter; for the summer feast upon soft berry fruits as in Blackcurrant Sorbet and Glazed Redcurrant and Raspberry Tart; the autumn will bring its rich bounty of apples, pears, nuts and hedge-row pickings so indulge in Discovery Dessert, Autumn Pudding and Baked Bramleys with Honey, Fruit and Walnut Filling; leaving winter with nursery favourites like Neapolitan Honey Pudding, Kishmish and Festive Cranberry Flan.

Above left: Apple and ginger squares (recipe page 144)
Below left: Banana and honey ice-cream (recipe page 144)
Below right: Honey and apricot college puddings (recipe page 144)

Apple and ginger squares

(Illustrated on pages 142–143)

175 g/6 oz (U.S. ¾ cup) butter or margarine
175 g/6 oz (U.S. 1 cup) light muscovado sugar
3 eggs
1 tablespoon clear honey
225 g/8 oz self-raising flour (U.S. 2 cups self-rising
flour sifted with 2 teaspoons baking powder)
1½ teaspoons ground ginger
½ teaspoon ground cinnamon
450 g/1 lb cooking apples, peeled, cored and chopped
Topping
150 ml/¼ pint double cream (U.S. ⅔ cup heavy cream)
¼ teaspoon ground cinnamon

Cream the butter or margarine and sugar in a bowl until light and fluffy. Beat in the eggs and honey, blending well.

Sift the flour with the ginger and cinnamon and fold into the creamed mixture with a metal spoon. Stir in the chopped apples, blending well.

Spoon into a greased and lined 20 cm/8 inch square cake tin. Bake in a preheated moderate oven (180°C, 350°F, Gas Mark 4) for 1½ hours until well-risen and golden.

Meanwhile, whip the cream with the cinnamon until it stands in soft peaks.

Cut the baked apple and ginger sponge into six squares to serve. Serve hot or cold with the cinnamon cream.
Serves 6

Banana and honey ice-cream

(Illustrated opposite and on pages 142–143)

450 g/1 lb bananas, peeled
150 ml/¼ pint double cream (U.S. ⅔ cup heavy cream)
150 ml/¼ pint (U.S. ⅔ cup) natural yogurt
2 tablespoons lemon juice
5 tablespoons (U.S. 6 tablespoons) set honey
50 g/2 oz (U.S. ½ cup) chopped nuts
2 egg whites

Mash the bananas until smooth. Add the cream, yogurt, lemon juice, honey and nuts, beating well to blend. Spoon into a shallow freezer tray and freeze until almost firm.

Scoop into a bowl and beat until smooth. Whisk the egg whites until they stand in stiff peaks. Fold into the ice-cream mixture with a metal spoon. Return to the freezer tray and freeze until firm, about 1–2 hours.

Remove from the freezer about 30 minutes before serving and leave to soften in the refrigerator. Scoop into chilled dessert glasses to serve with crisp biscuits (U.S. cookies). **Serves 6**

Honey and apricot college puddings

(Illustrated on pages 142–143)

100 g/4 oz (U.S. ⅔ cup) dried apricots, chopped
100 g/4 oz self-raising flour (U.S. 1 cup self-rising
flour sifted with 1 teaspoon baking powder)
1 teaspoon baking powder
100 g/4 oz castor sugar (U.S. ½ cup superfine sugar)
100 g/4 oz (U.S. ½ cup) soft blend margarine
2 large eggs (sizes 1, 2)
6 tablespoons (U.S. 7 tablespoons) clear honey
Sauce
100 g/4 oz (U.S. ⅔ cup) dried apricots, chopped
300 ml/½ pint (U.S. 1¼ cups) water
1 teaspoon lemon juice
50 g/2 oz (U.S. ⅓ cup) brown sugar

To make the puddings, place the apricots, flour, baking powder, sugar, margarine and eggs in a bowl. Beat well with a wooden spoon for 2–3 minutes.

Spoon the honey equally into six greased individual pudding moulds or a 900 ml/1½ pint pudding basin (U.S. 3¾ cup pudding mold). Top with the pudding mixture. Cover with a piece of pleated greaseproof paper (U.S. waxed paper) or greased foil, secure with string. Stand the individual puddings in a baking tin half-full with hot water.

Bake in a preheated moderately hot oven (190°C, 375°F, Gas Mark 5) for about 45–50 minutes. Steam the large pudding in a pan over simmering water for about 1½ hours.

To make the sauce, place the apricots and water in a pan and cook gently until tender, about 30 minutes. Stir in the lemon juice and sugar, blending well. Reserving a few apricots for decoration, purée the remainder in a blender or food processor.

Serve the sauce hot with the puddings, decorated with sliced apricot. **Serves 6**

Left: Banana and honey ice-cream
Right: Blackcurrant sorbet

Blackcurrant sorbet

(Illustrated above)

450 ml/¾ pint (U.S. 2 cups) water
thinly pared rind and juice of ½ lemon
200 g/7 oz sugar cubes
300 ml/½ pint (U.S. 1¼ cups) sieved blackcurrant purée
2 egg whites
mint leaves to decorate

Place the water, lemon rind and sugar in a pan. Bring slowly to the boil to dissolve the sugar then simmer for 5 minutes. Allow to cool, then remove and discard the lemon rind.

Add the lemon juice and blackcurrant purée, blending well. Pour into freezer trays and freeze until half-frozen.

Whisk the egg whites until they stand in stiff peaks and fold into the half-frozen mixture. Return to the freezer trays and freeze until firm.

Serve scooped into chilled glasses, decorated with mint leaves. **Serves 4–6**

Honey bread and butter pudding

25 g/1 oz (U.S. 2 tablespoons) butter
4 large slices bread, crusts removed
6 tablespoons (U.S. 7 tablespoons) creamed or set honey
25 g/1 oz sultanas (U.S. 3 tablespoons golden raisins), soaked in water
250 ml/8 fl oz single cream (U.S. 1 cup light cream)
200 ml/7 fl oz (U.S. ⅞ cup) milk
few drops of vanilla essence (U.S. extract)
2 eggs
dash of lemon juice

Butter the bread and spread with 2 teaspoons of honey. Cut slices into quarters. Place in buttered 1 litre/1¾–2 pint ovenproof dish. Drain sultanas, sprinkle over bread.

Heat the cream and milk to just below boiling point. Beat the eggs with the remaining honey and lemon juice. Stir into the milk mixture and strain over the bread.

Place the dish in a roasting tin half-filled with boiling water. Bake in a preheated moderate oven (160°C, 325°F, Gas Mark 3) for about 45 minutes until lightly set. Serve warm or cold. **Serves 4–6**

Honey and orange grape flan

(Illustrated above and on back cover)

Pastry
75 g/3 oz (U.S. 6 tablespoons) butter or margarine
175 g/6 oz plain flour (U.S. 1½ cups all-purpose flour)
40 g/1½ oz castor sugar (U.S. 3 tablespoons firmly
packed superfine sugar)
2 egg yolks
1 tablespoon cold water
Filling
25 g/1 oz (U.S. 2 tablespoons) butter
25 g/1 oz plain flour (U.S. ¼ cup all-purpose flour)
300 ml/½ pint (U.S. 1¼ cups) milk
25 g/1 oz castor sugar (U.S. 2 tablespoons firmly
packed superfine sugar)
1 egg yolk
1 tablespoon single cream (U.S. light cream)
1 tablespoon orange liqueur (optional)
Topping
3 oranges, peeled, pith removed and sliced
100 g/4 oz (U.S. 1 cup) green grapes
4 tablespoons (U.S. 5 tablespoons) clear honey

To make the pastry, rub the butter into the flour in a bowl until the mixture resembles fine breadcrumbs. Stir in the sugar, mix well. Mix egg yolks with the water and stir into mixture. Bind to make a firm dough.

Roll out on a lightly floured surface to a round large enough to line a 20 cm/8 inch fluted flan tin. Line with greaseproof paper (U.S. waxed paper) and fill with baking beans. Bake 'blind' in a preheated moderately hot oven (200°C, 400°F, Gas Mark 6) for 15–20 minutes. Remove the paper and beans and bake for a further 5–10 minutes or until cooked and golden. Cool on a wire rack.

To make the filling, melt the butter in a pan. Stir in the flour and cook for 1 minute. Remove from the heat and gradually add the milk, blending well. Bring to the boil and cook for 2–3 minutes, stirring until smooth.

Cool slightly then add the sugar, egg yolk, cream and liqueur. Pour into the flan base, leave to cool and set.

Decoratively arrange the orange slices and grapes over the filling. Brush with the honey. Chill. **Serves 6**

Lime crème

(Illustrated above)

225 g/8 oz (U.S. ¾ cup) lime curd
300 ml/½ pint double cream (U.S. 1¼ cups heavy cream)
2 egg whites
lime slices to decorate

Place the lime curd in a bowl. Whip the cream until it stands in soft peaks, fold into the lime curd, blend well.

Whisk the egg whites until they stand in stiff peaks. Fold in the lime mixture with a metal spoon.

Spoon into individual dessert glasses and decorate with slices of lime. Serve lightly chilled. **Serves 4**

Autumn pudding

(Illustrated above)

10 large slices wholewheat bread, crusts removed
225 g/8 oz gooseberries, topped and tailed
225 g/8 oz plums, stoned (U.S. pitted) and
coarsely chopped
225 g/8 oz cherries, stoned (U.S. pitted)
225 g/8 oz blackberries, hulled
100–150 ml/4–5 fl oz (U.S. $\frac{1}{3}$–$\frac{1}{2}$ cup) clear honey
1$\frac{1}{2}$ teaspoons agar powder
natural yogurt to serve

Use eight slices of the bread to line the base and sides of a
1.2 litre/2 pint pudding basin (U.S. 5 cup pudding mold).

Place the gooseberries, plums, cherries, blackberries
and 100 ml/4 fl oz (U.S. $\frac{1}{3}$ cup) of the honey in a pan. Cook
over a gentle heat until tender, about 8–10 minutes.
Sweeten with extra honey if liked.

Spoon a few tablespoons of the juice over the bread in
the basin to moisten it and hold it in place. Spoon the
fruit into the basin reserving the juice in the pan.

Sprinkle the agar powder over the reserved juice and
heat gently until dissolved. Pour over the fruit.

Use the remaining bread to make a lid for the fruit,
cutting to fit as necessary. Cover loosely with a disc of
greaseproof paper or cling film (U.S. waxed paper or
Saran wrap) and weight down. Chill overnight or for
6–8 hours. To serve, unmould the pudding on to a serving plate. Serve with a little natural yogurt. **Serves 6**

Indian banana and satsuma pudding

(Illustrated above)

2 teaspoons sugar
$\frac{1}{2}$ teaspoon ground black pepper
$\frac{1}{2}$ teaspoon chilli powder (U.S. chili powder)
1 teaspoon salt
300 ml/$\frac{1}{2}$ pint (U.S. 1$\frac{1}{4}$ cups) natural yogurt
2 large bananas, peeled and thinly sliced
2 large satsumas (U.S. tangerines), peeled and
segmented
$\frac{1}{2}$ teaspoon saffron
1 teaspoon water

Mix the sugar with the pepper, chilli powder, salt and
yogurt, blending well.

Add the bananas and satsumas, mixing well to blend.

Soak the saffron in the water and sprinkle over the
prepared dessert just before serving. **Serves 4**

Discovery dessert

(Illustrated below)

225 g/8 oz (U.S. 1 cup firmly packed) granulated sugar
300 ml/½ pint (U.S. 1¼ cups) water
piece of pared lemon rind
1.8 kg/4 lb Discovery dessert apples, peeled, cored
and thinly sliced
50 g/2 oz chopped mixed peel (U.S. ⅓ cup chopped
candied peel)
50 g/2 oz sultanas (U.S. ⅓ cup golden raisins) or
seedless raisins
To decorate
whipped cream
apple slices

Place the sugar, water and lemon rind in a large pan. Bring to the boil, add the apples and cook gently until just transparent.

Remove the apple slices carefully with a slotted spoon and place a layer in the base of a foil-lined 18 cm/7 inch round cake tin. Spinkle with a little peel and sultanas or raisins. Continue layering in this way until all the ingredients have been used. Chill thoroughly.

To serve, turn out carefully on to a serving plate. Decorate with swirls of whipped cream and slices of apple. Cut into wedges to serve. **Serves 6–8**

Variations
Layered pear dessert Prepare and cook as before but use 1.8 kg/4 lb firm dessert pears instead of the Discovery apples. Peel, core and thinly slice and cook gently as above until just tender and transparent but not fallen.
Spiced Discovery dessert Prepare and cook as before but sprinkle the apple slices with a little ground cinnamon, nutmeg or ginger (or a mixture as ground mixed spice) when layering with the mixed peel and sultanas or raisins. Alternatively, decorate the dessert with swirls of spice-flavoured cream. Whip about 300 ml/½ pint double cream (U.S. 1¼ cups heavy cream) with about 1 teaspoon of the chosen spice until it stands in soft peaks.

Pippin pies

(Illustrated below)

Pastry
450 g/1 lb plain flour (U.S. 4 cups all-purpose flour)
275 g/10 oz (U.S. 1¼ cups) butter or margarine
75 g/3 oz castor sugar (U.S. 6 tablespoons firmly
packed superfine sugar)
1 egg, beaten
cold water to bind
Filling
75 g/3 oz (U.S. 6 tablespoons) butter
40 g/1½ oz castor sugar (U.S. 3 tablespoons firmly
packed superfine sugar)
pinch of ground cloves
grated rind of 1 large orange
6 Cox's Orange Pippin dessert apples, peeled and
cored
beaten egg to glaze
castor sugar (U.S. superfine sugar) to dust

To make the pastry, sift the flour into a bowl. Rub in (U.S. cut in) the butter or margarine until the mixture resembles fine breadcrumbs. Stir in the sugar, egg and sufficient water to bind to a firm but pliable dough. Chill for 30 minutes.

Meanwhile to make the filling, cream the butter with the sugar, cloves and orange rind. Fill the centres of the apples with the mixture.

Roll out the pastry on a lightly floured surface and cut into six 15 cm/6 inch squares. Place an apple in the centre of each, dampen the pastry edges and draw the pastry around the apples to completely enclose. Place on a greased baking tray and glaze with beaten egg. Sprinkle with a little sugar.

Bake in a preheated moderately hot oven (200°C, 400°F, Gas Mark 6) for 15 minutes. Reduce the oven temperature to moderate (160°C, 325°F, Gas Mark 3) and bake for a further 15–20 minutes.

Serve hot or cold with whipped or pouring cream.
Makes 6

Baked Bramleys with honey, fruit and walnut filling

(Illustrated above)

4 medium Bramley apples (U.S. tart cooking apples)
50 g/2 oz sultanas (U.S. $\frac{1}{3}$ cup golden raisins)
25 g/1 oz chopped mixed peel (U.S. 3 tablespoons chopped candied peel)
25 g/1 oz (U.S. $\frac{1}{4}$ cup) walnuts, chopped
4 tablespoons (U.S. 5 tablespoons) clear honey

Wipe the apples with a damp cloth and remove the cores, making a fairly large cavity. Slit the skin with the point of a sharp knife around the centre of each apple to prevent them from bursting during cooking.

Mix the sultanas with the peel, walnuts and sufficient honey to bind. Stuff the apple cavities with the honey mixture and place in a buttered shallow ovenproof dish.

Pour in 1 cm/$\frac{1}{2}$ inch water and spoon the remaining honey over the apples.

Cover with buttered greaseproof paper (U.S. waxed paper). Bake in a preheated moderate oven (180°C, 350°F, Gas Mark 4) for about 30–45 minutes until tender but not fallen.

Baste with the honey juices to serve. Serve hot with fresh cream. **Serves 4**

Variations

Baked Bramleys with honey, muesli and walnut filling Prepare and cook as before but stuff the apples with a mixture of 75 g/3 oz (U.S. 1 cup) muesli mixed with 4 teaspoons clear honey and the juice of 1 lemon. Decorate with walnut halves to serve.

Baked Bramleys with honey, fruit and coconut filling Prepare and cook as before but use 2 tablespoons toasted long-thread coconut instead of the chopped mixed peel.

Vacherin aux marrons

(Illustrated above)

4 egg whites
225 g/8 oz castor sugar (U.S. 1 cup superfine sugar)
$\frac{1}{2}$ teaspoon vanilla essence (U.S. vanilla flavoring)
100 g/4 oz (U.S. 1 cup) ground hazelnuts
Filling
225 g/8 oz (U.S. scant 1 cup) canned chestnut purée
50 g/2 oz icing sugar (U.S. $\frac{1}{2}$ cup confectioner's sugar), sifted
2 tablespoons dark rum
150 ml/$\frac{1}{4}$ pint double cream (U.S. $\frac{2}{3}$ cup heavy cream), whipped
To decorate
150 ml/$\frac{1}{4}$ pint double cream (U.S. $\frac{2}{3}$ cup heavy cream), whipped
25 g/1 oz plain chocolate (U.S. 1 square semi-sweet chocolate), coarsely grated or curled
25 g/1 oz (U.S. $\frac{1}{4}$ cup) hazelnuts, coarsely chopped

Whisk the egg whites until they stand in stiff peaks. Whisk in the sugar, a little at a time, until thick and glossy. Fold in the vanilla and nuts with a metal spoon.

Divide between two greased and base-lined 20 cm/ 8 inch sandwich tins (U.S. layer cake pans) and level the surfaces. Bake in a preheated moderate oven (180°C, 350°F, Gas Mark 4) for 35–40 minutes or until crisp and lightly coloured on top. Allow to cool on a wire rack.

Meanwhile to make the filling, beat the chestnut purée with the icing sugar and rum until smooth. Fold in the whipped cream. Sandwich the meringue rounds together with half of the chestnut mixture and place on a serving plate.

Spread the remaining chestnut mixture over the top of the cake. Place the cream to decorate in a piping bag (U.S. pastry bag) fitted with a large star nozzle and pipe swirls around the top edge of the cake.

Sprinkle the chestnut filling with the chocolate and nuts. Serve as soon as possible. **Serves 6**

Glazed redcurrant and raspberry tart

(Illustrated below)

Pastry
125 g/4½ oz plain flour (U.S. 1 cup plus 2 tablespoons all-purpose flour)
pinch of salt
75 g/3 oz (U.S. 6 tablespoons) unsalted butter
1½ tablespoons castor sugar (U.S. superfine sugar)
about 2 teaspoons cold water
Filling
150 g/5 oz (U.S. ⅔ cup) low-fat soft cheese
1 × 150 g/5 oz jar redcurrant sauce
225 g/8 oz (U.S. 1½ cups) raspberries, hulled

To make the pastry, sift the flour and salt into a bowl. Rub in (U.S. cut in) the butter until the mixture resembles fine breadcrumbs. Stir in the sugar and water and bind to a firm dough.

Roll out the pastry on a lightly floured surface to a round large enough to line a greased 19 cm/7½ inch fluted flan tin. Chill for 15 minutes.

Prick the base, line with greaseproof paper (U.S. waxed paper) and fill with baking beans. Bake 'blind' in a pre-heated moderately hot oven (200°C, 400°F, Gas Mark 6) for 20 minutes. Remove the baking beans and paper and cook for a further 5 minutes. Allow to cool, remove from the tin and place on a serving plate.

To make the filling, blend the cheese with 2 tablespoons of the redcurrant sauce and spread over the base of the flan. Arrange the raspberries on top of the cheese filling.

Warm the remaining redcurrant sauce and, using a pastry brush, glaze the raspberries. Chill lightly before serving. **Serves 6**

Neapolitan honey pudding

(Illustrated below)

75 g/3 oz (U.S. 6 tablespoons) soft blend margarine
100 g/4 oz (U.S. $\frac{1}{3}$ cup) clear honey
2 eggs
175 g/6 oz (U.S. $1\frac{1}{2}$ cups) plain wholewheat flour
1 teaspoon baking powder
50 g/2 oz glacé cherries (U.S. $\frac{1}{4}$ cup candied cherries), quartered
50 g/2 oz (U.S. $\frac{1}{3}$ cup) chopped mixed peel
50 g/2 oz (U.S. $\frac{1}{3}$ cup) chocolate chips or polka dots
50 g/2 oz (U.S. $\frac{1}{2}$ cup) walnuts, chopped
1 tablespoon milk

Place the margarine, honey, eggs, flour and baking powder in a bowl and beat to blend, about 2–3 minutes.

Add the cherries, peel, chocolate chips, walnuts and milk and beat for a further 1 minute.

Spoon into a greased 1.2 litre/2 pint pudding basin (U.S. 5 cup pudding mold) and cover with a piece of pleated, greased foil.

Place in a large saucepan and pour boiling water around to come half-way up the sides. Cover and simmer gently for $1\frac{1}{2}$–2 hours until cooked, adding more boiling water if necessary.

Turn out on to a warmed plate to serve. Serve at once with custard or cream. **Serves 4–6**

Variation
Neapolitan syrup pudding Prepare and cook as before but substitute golden or corn syrup for the honey. If liked the walnuts in either the honey or the syrup version may be replaced with pecans, hazelnuts or almonds and the glacé cherries replaced with any other crystallized or glacé fruits like pineapple, nectarines, apricots or peaches including marrons glacés (crystallized or glacé chestnuts).

153

Festive cranberry flan

Pastry
175 g/6 oz plain flour (U.S. 1½ cups all-purpose flour)
100 g/4 oz (U.S. ½ cup) butter
25 g/1 oz castor sugar (U.S. 2 tablespoons superfine
sugar)
1 tablespoon water
Filling
75 g/3 oz (U.S. ½ cup) raisins
75 g/3 oz (U.S. ½ cup) currants
50 g/2 oz chopped mixed peel (U.S. ⅓ cup chopped
candied peel)
50 g/2 oz (U.S. ½ cup) walnuts, chopped
1 × 175 g/6 oz jar cranberry sauce with wine
25 g/1 oz (U.S. 2 tablespoons) butter, melted
sifted icing sugar (U.S. confectioner's sugar) to dust

To make the pastry, sift the flour into a bowl. Rub in
(U.S. cut in) the butter until the mixture resembles fine
breadcrumbs. Stir in the sugar and water and bind to a
firm dough.

Roll out the pastry on a lightly floured surface to a
round large enough to line a greased 20 cm/8 inch French
fluted flan tin. Reserve the trimmings and use to cut out
two Christmas trees for the decoration. Prick the base,
line with greaseproof paper (U.S. waxed paper) and fill
with baking beans. Bake 'blind' in a preheated moderately
hot oven (200°C, 400°F, Gas Mark 6) for 20–25 minutes.

To make the filling, mix the raisins with the currants,
peel, walnuts, cranberry sauce and butter, blending well.

Remove the baking beans and paper. Spoon the fruit
filling into the partly-cooked flan. Top with the pastry
Christmas trees.

Reduce the oven temperature to moderate (180°C,
350°F, Gas Mark 4) and continue to cook for 15–20
minutes. Cool slightly then remove from the tin.

Dust the Christmas trees lightly with sugar. Serve
warm or cold with cream. **Serves 4–6**

Kishmish

(Illustrated above)

450 g/1 lb mixed dried fruits
4 tablespoons (U.S. 5 tablespoons) clear honey
4 tablespoons (U.S. 5 tablespoons) brandy
4 tablespoons (U.S. 5 tablespoons) water
1 stick cinnamon
3 cloves
¼ teaspoon ground allspice
strip of pared lemon rind

Soak the fruits overnight or for at least 4 hours in cold
water. Drain thoroughly.

Place the fruit in a pan with the honey, brandy, water,
cinnamon, cloves, allspice and lemon rind. Bring to the
boil, reduce the heat and simmer gently for 10 minutes.
Allow to cool, then chill thoroughly.

Serve in individual glass dishes with whipped cream
or ice-cream. **Serves 2**

Honey puffs Zalabia

225 g/8 oz plain flour (U.S. 2 cups all-purpose flour)
7 g/¼ oz dried yeast (U.S. active dry yeast)
1 teaspoon sugar
300 ml/½ pint (U.S. 1¼ cups) warm milk and water mixed
oil for deep frying

Syrup
5 tablespoons (U.S. 6 tablespoons) set honey
200 ml/7 fl oz (U.S. ⅞ cup) water
1 tablespoon lemon juice
1 tablespoon rose water (optional)
candied orange peel strips to decorate

Sift the flour into a bowl. Dissolve the yeast and sugar in the milk and water. Leave to stand in a warm place until frothy, about 15 minutes.

Make a well in the flour and pour in the yeast mixture. Using a wooden spoon, beat to form a smooth, soft batter. Cover and leave to rise in a warm place for 1 hour. Beat well, cover and prove for 1 hour. Repeat once.

Meanwhile to make the syrup, mix the honey and water in a pan. Add the lemon juice and rose water if used. Stir over a gentle heat until well mixed. Cool.

Heat the oil in a pan to 190°C, 375°F or until a cube of bread browns in 1 minute. Shape small teaspoonfuls of the dough with a wet spoon and drop into the hot oil. Fry gently, a few at a time, until crisp and golden on all sides. Remove with a slotted spoon and drain.

Dip in the syrup and place in a serving dish. Decorate and serve with cream. **Serves 4–6**

Pear upside-down cake

(Illustrated above)

Topping
1 tablespoon lemon juice
3 tablespoons (U.S. 4 tablespoons) light brown sugar
50 g/2 oz (U.S. ¼ cup) butter
6 glacé cherries (U.S. candied cherries)
1 × 410 g/14½ oz can pear halves, drained

Base
2 eggs
100 g/4 oz castor sugar (U.S. ½ cup superfine sugar)
150 g/5 oz self-raising flour (U.S. 1¼ cups self-rising
flour sifted with 1 teaspoon baking powder)
100 g/4 oz (U.S. ½ cup) soft blend margarine
2 tablespoons lemon juice

To make the topping, mix the lemon juice with the sugar and butter. Use to coat the bottom of a 25 cm/10 inch base-lined shallow round cake tin. Place a cherry in each pear half and arrange, cherry side and cut-side down, in the tin.

To make the base, place the eggs, sugar, flour, margarine and lemon juice in a bowl and beat until light and fluffy, about 3 minutes. Spread over the fruit, levelling the surface.

Bake in a preheated moderate oven (180°C, 350°F, Gas Mark 4) for 45 minutes.

Turn out on to a warmed plate and serve hot with cream or custard. **Serves 6**

Honey, yogurt and dried fruit pancakes

(Illustrated below and on the front cover)

Pancakes
50 g/2 oz (U.S. ½ cup) wholewheat flour
50 g/2 oz plain flour (U.S. ½ cup all-purpose flour)
pinch of salt
1 egg
1 egg yolk
300 ml/½ pint (U.S. 1¼ cups) milk
about 2–3 tablespoons oil
Filling
225 g/8 oz (U.S. 1⅓ cups) mixed dried fruit
4 tablespoons (U.S. 5 tablespoons) clear honey
2 tablespoons water
2 tablespoons lemon juice
300 ml/½ pint (U.S. 1¼ cups) natural yogurt
extra honey to drizzle

To make the pancake batter, mix the flours and salt in a bowl. Make a well in the centre and add the egg and egg yolk. Gradually draw the flour into the egg mixture to make a smooth batter, adding the milk and 1 tablespoon of the oil. Cover and leave to stand for 30 minutes.

Smear a 20 cm/8 inch frying pan (U.S. skillet) with a little of the oil and heat until hot. When hot, pour in just enough batter to cover the base of the pan. Cook until the underside is golden, then turn over with a spatula and cook the second side. Transfer to a plate, cover with a sheet of greaseproof paper (U.S. waxed paper) and repeat with the remaining batter to make about 12–14 pancakes. Keep warm.

Meanwhile to make the filling, place the dried fruit, honey, water and lemon juice in a pan and bring to the boil. Reduce the heat and simmer until the fruit is tender and the syrup is reduced by half.

Spoon the filling on to the pancakes. Roll up and arrange, seam-side down, on a warmed serving dish. Spoon over the yogurt and drizzle with honey to finish.
Serves 6

Scotch pancakes with lemon butter

(Illustrated below)

Pancakes
100 g/4 oz self-raising flour (U.S. 1 cup self-rising flour
sifted with 1 teaspoon baking powder)
25 g/1 oz castor sugar (U.S. 2 tablespoons firmly packed
superfine sugar)
1 egg, beaten
2 tablespoons lemon juice
5 tablespoons (U.S. 6 tablespoons) milk
a little melted butter
Lemon Butter
100 g/4 oz (U.S. $\frac{1}{2}$ cup) butter
75 g/3 oz icing sugar (U.S. $\frac{3}{4}$ cup confectioner's sugar),
sifted
2 tablespoons lemon juice
natural yogurt to serve

To make the pancake batter, sift the flour into a bowl and stir in the sugar. Make a well in the centre of the mixture and add the egg. Add the lemon juice and 2 tablespoons of the milk. Beat until well mixed, then gradually add the remaining milk to make a smooth batter.

Heat a griddle or frying pan (U.S. skillet) over moderate heat and brush lightly with a little melted butter. Drop tablespoons of the batter on to the heated griddle or frying pan and cook for about 2 minutes, or until bubbles appear and a 'skin' forms on the surface of the pancakes. Turn over carefully with a spatula and continue to cook for 1–2 minutes, or until the second side is golden. Keep warm.

Meanwhile to make the lemon butter, beat the butter until pale and fluffy. Beat in the sugar, a little at a time, with the lemon juice until smooth.

Spread the lemon butter over the pancakes. Serve warm with a little natural yogurt. **Serves 4–6**

Baking

The sizzling sound of scones, plain, fruited or savoury, on a griddle; the soothing hiss of fruit baked pastry pies cooling in their dishes; and the rising splendour to great heights of home-baked yeasted breads as they prove in the bowl are the joys of home baking in all its glory. Whether your repertoire simply starts and stops with making the occasional rare special cake or your weekly ritual includes several bread-making sessions alongside cake, pastry and teabread cook-ins, your needs are catered for in this section.

You'll find many of the tried and trusted basics like Wholewheat Bread, Wholewheat Sponge, Honey Gingerbread and Sesame Flap-jacks alongside new tempting soon-to-become favourites like Lemon Honey Cake, Carrot and Pecan Loaf and Bran, Hazelnut and Oat Slice.

As can be expected many are teatime special-ities like Orange Curd Bakewells and Whole-some Barm Brack but others like Apricot Lattice Tart and Honey Walnut Roulade would make a delicious worthy pudding or dessert. Consider Almond Shortbread Fingers as light dessert biscuits, Soft Honey Cookies and Crunchy Ginger Bars for lunchbox fare and Carob Cream Cake as an indulgent 'coffee or elevenses' mid-morning treat.

Store most carefully in an airtight tin for fresh-ness and, when time affords the luxury, make in bulk and freeze away to enjoy at a later date. Refresh quickly in a hot oven for same-day-baked freshness if possible or freeze uncooked then defrost thoroughly before baking.

Top: *Wholewheat sponge (recipe page 165)*
Centre left: *Wholewheat walnut scones (recipe page 160)*
Centre right: *Wholewheat bread (recipe page 160)*
Below: *Apricot lattice tart (recipe page 162)*

Wholewheat bread

(Illustrated opposite and on pages 158–159)

675 g/1½ lb wholewheat flour
1 teaspoon salt
25 g/1 oz fresh yeast (U.S. 1 cake compressed yeast)
1 teaspoon molasses
450 ml/¾ pint (U.S. 2 cups) warm water
1 tablespoon sunflower oil
buckwheat, cracked wheat, seeds and nuts to
sprinkle (optional)

Mix the flour with the salt in a large bowl.

Cream the yeast with the molasses and 150 ml/¼ pint of the water. Leave in a warm place until frothy, about 5 minutes.

Add the yeast liquid, remaining water and the oil to the flour mixture and mix to a smooth dough. Turn the dough on to a lightly floured surface and knead until smooth and elastic, about 10 minutes. Place in an oiled bowl, cover with cling film (U.S. Saran wrap) and leave to rise in a warm place until doubled in size, about 1½–2 hours.

Turn the dough on to a lightly floured surface, knock back (U.S. punch down) to release all the air bubbles and knead for about 5 minutes. Shape into loaves or rolls as follows:

Tin loaf Flatten the dough out to an oblong about 2.5 cm/1 inch thick. Fold in three and tuck the ends over the seam. Place, seam side down, in a greased 1 kg/2 lb loaf tin.

Split tin Prepare as Tin Loaf but make a deep slit lengthways down the centre of the loaf with a sharp knife.

Cob Knead the dough into a ball by drawing the dough upwards and into the centre. Place tucks side down on a greased baking tray.

Crown loaf Divide the dough into twelve equal pieces and knead each into a small ball. Place slightly apart in a large, greased, shallow round tin. Place about nine around the outside edge of the tin and three in the centre.

Plait Divide the dough into three equal pieces. Roll each into a long strand. Starting at the centre, plait the strands loosely together down to one end. Dampen the end of each strand with water and pinch together to seal. Plait the remaining end in the same way.

Cottage loaf Cut off one third of the dough. Knead each piece of dough into a ball. Place the larger round on a greased baking tray and flatten slightly on top. Place the smaller ball on top. Push a floured wooden spoon handle through both the top and the bottom balls of dough to make a hole in the centre of the loaf.

Round rolls Divide the dough into twelve equal pieces. Shape into rounds and place well apart on greased baking trays.

Cloverleaf rolls Divide the dough into twelve equal pieces then divide each portion again into three pieces. Shape each piece into a small ball. Place in groups of three in greased Yorkshire pudding tins or on large greased baking trays.

Daisy wheel rolls Divide the dough into twelve equal pieces. Shape into rounds and place well apart on greased baking trays. Slash the sides of the rolls in five places, radiating from the centre to make daisy wheels.

Crescents Divide the dough into twelve equal pieces and roll out each piece into a large flat square shape. Roll up from one corner to the diagonally opposite corner to make crescent shapes and twist gently to make 'horns'.

Cover the dough with cling film (U.S. Saran wrap) and leave in a warm place to prove until the dough has risen to double its original size, about 15–30 minutes. Sprinkle with buckwheat, cracked wheat, seeds or nuts if liked.

Bake in a preheated hot oven (220°C, 425°F, Gas Mark 7) until cooked. Large loaves will take 35–40 minutes, small loaves will take 20–30 minutes and rolls will take 15–20 minutes. When cooked, the loaves or rolls should sound hollow when rapped on the bottom with the knuckles. Allow to cool on a wire rack.

Makes about 900 g/2 lb

Wholewheat walnut scones

(Illustrated on pages 158–159)

100 g/4 oz plain white flour (U.S. 1 cup all-purpose flour)
4 teaspoons baking powder
pinch of salt
pinch of cayenne pepper
100 g/4 oz (U.S. 1 cup) wholewheat flour
50 g/2 oz (U.S. ¼ cup) margarine
75 g/3 oz (U.S. ¾ cup) walnuts, finely chopped
100 g/4 oz (U.S. ¼ lb) Summer Orchard cereal
about 175 ml/6 fl oz (U.S. ¾ cup) skimmed milk

Sift the white flour, baking powder, salt and cayenne pepper into a bowl. Blend in the wholewheat flour.

Rub in (U.S. cut in) the margarine until the mixture resembles fine breadcrumbs. Stir in the walnuts, cereal and milk. Mix to a soft but not sticky dough.

Divide the dough into twelve pieces and shape each into a ball. Place in a lightly greased 18 cm/7 inch sandwich tin (U.S. layer cake pan) and glaze with a little milk. Bake in a preheated moderately hot oven (200°C, 400°F, Gas Mark 6) for about 25 minutes.

Allow to cool on a wire rack. Serve warm or cold with butter and jam if liked. **Makes 12**

***From the top clockwise:** Wholewheat bread – plait, tin loaf, cloverleaf rolls, crescents, daisy wheel rolls, split tin, cottage loaf, crown loaf, round rolls*

Apricot lattice tart

(Illustrated above and on pages 158–159)

225 g/8 oz (U.S. 2 cups) wholewheat flour
$\frac{1}{4}$ teaspoon salt
50 g/2 oz (U.S. $\frac{1}{4}$ cup) butter or margarine
50 g/2 oz (U.S. $\frac{1}{4}$ cup) vegetable fat
3–4 tablespoons iced water
Filling
2 × 425 g/15 oz cans apricot halves in fruit juice or
water, drained
100 g/4 oz demerara sugar ((U.S. $\frac{1}{2}$ cup brown sugar)
1 teaspoon ground mixed spice
beaten egg to glaze

To make the pastry, mix the flour with the salt in a bowl. Rub the butter or margarine and vegetable fat into the flour until the mixture resembles fine breadcrumbs. Add water and bind to a firm pliable dough.

Roll out the pastry on a lightly floured surface to a round large enough to line a greased 18 cm/7 inch flan ring set on a baking tray. Prick the base with a fork.

Fill the flan with the apricots, placed cut side down – this quantity will give a two-layer filling of apricots. Sprinkle with the sugar and mixed spice.

Roll out the pastry trimmings and cut, using a fluted pastry wheel if liked, into about six long thin strips. Place on the tart to make a lattice. Glaze with egg.

Bake in a preheated moderately hot oven (190°C, 375°F, Gas Mark 5) for about 30 minutes. Serve hot or cold with pouring custard or cream. **Serves 6**

Honey muffins

(Illustrated above and on page 6)

450 g/1 lb wholewheat flour
1 teaspoon salt
1 sachet Easy Bake Yeast
100 ml/4 fl oz (U.S. $\frac{1}{2}$ cup) milk
100 ml/4 fl oz (U.S. $\frac{1}{2}$ cup) water
50 g/2 oz (U.S. 3 tablespoons) clear honey
1 egg, beaten
25 g/1 oz (U.S. 2 tablespoons) butter, melted

Mix the flour, salt and yeast in a large bowl.

Place the milk, water and honey in a pan and heat until lukewarm (43°C/110°F).

Add to the flour mixture with the egg and butter and mix to a soft dough. Turn the dough on to a lightly floured surface and knead until smooth and elastic, about 5 minutes. Return to the bowl, cover and leave to rise in a warm place until increased in size by half, 15 minutes.

Roll out the dough on a lightly floured surface to about 1 cm/$\frac{1}{2}$ inch thick. Stamp out rounds using a 7.5 cm/3 inch scone cutter, re-rolling as necessary.

Dust two baking trays with a little flour. Place the muffins on the trays and cover loosely with polythene. Prove in a warm place until well risen, 30 minutes.

Sprinkle with a little more flour or ground rice. Bake in a preheated moderately hot oven (200°C, 400°F, Gas Mark 6) for about 10 minutes, turning over halfway. Cool on a wire rack. Serve warm or cold, split and buttered and spread with set honey. **Makes 8–12**

Almond shortbread fingers

(Illustrated above)

200 g/7 oz plain flour (U.S. 1¾ cups all-purpose flour)
25 g/1 oz (U.S. ¼ cup) ground rice
150 g/5 oz (U.S. ½ cup plus 2 tablespoons) butter
50 g/2 oz (U.S. ⅓ cup) blanched almonds, chopped
25 g/1 oz (U.S. 3 tablespoons) chopped mixed peel
75 g/3 oz castor sugar (U.S. 6 tablespoons superfine sugar)
few drops of almond essence (U.S. almond extract)

Sift the flour and ground rice into a bowl. Rub in (U.S. cut in) the butter until the mixture resembles fine bread-crumbs. Stir in the almonds, peel, sugar and almond essence, blending well. Knead the mixture well to form a ball.

Press into a greased 28 × 18 cm/11 × 7 inch shallow tin. Prick with a fork.

Bake in a preheated moderate oven (180 °C, 350 °F, Gas Mark 4) for 30 minutes until golden. Using a sharp knife, mark into fingers while still hot.

Allow to cool in the tin. Remove from the tin with a palette knife (U.S. spatula) to serve.
Makes about 20 fingers

Spiced coconut cookies

(Illustrated above)

100 g/4 oz (U.S. ½ cup) butter or margarine
100 g/4 oz (U.S. ⅔ cup) light muscovado sugar
1 egg
100 g/4 oz self-raising Farmhouse flour (U.S. 1 cup self-rising flour sifted with 1 teaspoon baking powder)
pinch of salt
½ teaspoon ground cinnamon
½ teaspoon ground mixed spice
75 g/3 oz desiccated coconut (U.S. 1 cup shredded coconut)

Cream the butter or margarine with the sugar and egg in a bowl until light and fluffy. Fold in the flour, salt, cinnamon, ground mixed spice and coconut, blending well.

Place heaped teaspoonfuls of the mixture on to two greased baking trays, spacing about 5 cm/2 inches apart.

Bake in a preheated moderate oven (180 °C, 350 °F, Gas Mark 4) until crisp and golden, about 20–25 minutes. Allow to cool on a wire rack. **Makes 24**

Wholewheat sponge

(Illustrated on pages 158–159)

175 g/6 oz (U.S. ¾ cup) butter or margarine
175 g/6 oz (U.S. 1 cup) soft brown sugar
3 eggs, beaten
175 g/6 oz self-raising wheatmeal flour (U.S. 1½ cups
self-rising wholewheat flour)
1 teaspoon baking powder
4 tablespoons (U.S. 5 tablespoons) jam
150 ml/¼ pint double cream (U.S. ⅔ cup heavy cream),
whipped
sifted icing sugar (U.S. confectioner's sugar) to dust
(optional)

Cream the butter or margarine with the sugar in a bowl until light and fluffy. Beat in the eggs with a little of the flour.

Mix the remaining flour with the baking powder and fold into the creamed mixture. Divide between two greased and base-lined 20 cm/8 inch sandwich tins (U.S. layer cake pans) and level the tops.

Bake in a preheated moderate oven (180°C, 350°F, Gas Mark 4) for 30–35 minutes or until the tops spring back when lightly touched with the fingertips. Leave to cool in the tins for 2–3 minutes, then transfer to a wire rack to cool completely.

When cold, sandwich the cakes together with jam and cream. Dust the top with sugar if liked. Cut into wedges to serve. **Serves 8**

Honey walnut roulade

(Illustrated opposite)

3 large eggs (sizes 1, 2), separated
2 teaspoons water
75 g/3 oz castor sugar (U.S. 6 tablespoons superfine
sugar)
2 tablespoons clear honey
100 g/4 oz self-raising flour (U.S. 1 cup self-rising flour
sifted with 1 teaspoon baking powder)
75 g/3 oz (U.S. ¾ cup) ground walnuts
Filling
300 ml/½ pint double cream (U.S. 1¼ cups heavy cream)
1 tablespoon clear honey
25 g/1 oz (U.S. ¼ cup) walnut pieces
walnut halves to decorate

Line a 24 × 28 cm/9½ × 11 inch Swiss roll tin (U.S. jelly roll pan) with greaseproof paper (U.S. waxed paper). Grease and dust with a little flour.

Whisk the egg whites with the water in a bowl until they stand in stiff peaks. Gradually add the sugar, a spoonful at a time and beat until stiff. Fold in the egg yolks and honey with a metal spoon, blending well.

Sift the flour and mix with the walnuts. Fold into the egg mixture with a metal spoon.

Spoon into the prepared tin and level the surface. Bake in a preheated moderately hot oven (200°C, 400°F, Gas Mark 6) for about 12 minutes or until firm to the touch.

Turn quickly on to a sugared sheet of greaseproof paper, using a sharp knife to trim away the crisp edges of the roulade and roll up, enclosing the paper. Allow to cool.

Meanwhile to make the filling, whip the cream until it stands in soft peaks. Remove one third and set aside. Fold the honey and walnut pieces into the remaining two thirds, blending well.

Unroll the roulade and remove the greaseproof paper. Spread with the honey and walnut cream and re-roll. Place, seamside down, on a serving dish.

Place the reserved cream in a piping bag (U.S. pastry bag) fitted with a star-shaped nozzle and pipe swirls of cream down the top of the roulade. Decorate with walnut halves and slice to serve. **Serves 6**

Honey gingerbread

(Illustrated opposite)

100 g/4 oz (U.S. ½ cup) butter or margarine
100 g/4 oz (U.S. ⅔ cup) brown sugar
4 tablespoons (U.S. 5 tablespoons) set honey
2 eggs, beaten
225 g/8 oz plain flour (U.S. 2 cups all-purpose
flour)
1 tablespoon ground ginger
1 teaspoon bicarbonate of soda (U.S. baking soda)
25 g/1 oz (U.S. 3 tablespoons) mixed dried fruit

Place the butter or margarine, sugar and honey in a pan and heat to melt. Remove from the heat and stir in the eggs, blending well.

Mix the flour with the ginger, bicarbonate of soda and dried fruit. Stir into the melted mixture and mix well to blend.

Spoon into a greased and lined 15 × 20 cm/6 × 8 inch tin and level the surface. Bake in a preheated moderate oven (180°C, 350°F, Gas Mark 4) for about 35 minutes or until springy to the touch. Turn out and allow to cool on a wire rack.

Store in an airtight tin until required. Cut into slices to serve. **Makes 1 × 15 × 20 cm/6 × 8 inch cake**

Above: Honey gingerbread
Below: Honey walnut roulade

Cherry and almond cake

(Illustrated below)

175 g/6 oz (U.S. $\frac{3}{4}$ cup) butter or margarine
175 g/6 oz (U.S. 1 cup) demerara sugar
3 eggs
100 g/4 oz plain flour (U.S. 1 cup all-purpose flour)
100 g/4 oz (U.S. 1 cup) plain wholewheat flour
50 g/2 oz (U.S. $\frac{1}{2}$ cup) ground almonds
1$\frac{1}{2}$ teaspoons baking powder
225 g/8 oz glacé cherries (U.S. 1 cup candied cherries),
halved

Cream the butter or margarine with the sugar in a bowl until light and fluffy. Gradually beat in the eggs, blending well.

Fold in the flours, ground almonds and baking powder, blending well. Finally stir in the cherries to mix.

Spoon into a greased and lined 18 cm/7 inch deep round cake tin and level the surface. Bake in a preheated moderate oven (160°C, 325°F, Gas Mark 3) for 1$\frac{3}{4}$–2 hours or until well risen and golden. Turn out and allow to cool on a wire rack. **Makes 1 × 18 cm/7 inch round cake**

Lemon honey cake

(Illustrated left)

100 g/4 oz (U.S. $\frac{1}{2}$ cup) butter or margarine
50 g/2 oz (U.S. 3 tablespoons) set honey
50 g/2 oz (U.S. $\frac{1}{3}$ cup) soft brown sugar
1 egg, beaten
grated rind and juice of 1 lemon
175 g/6 oz self-raising Farmhouse flour (U.S. 1$\frac{1}{2}$ cups self-rising wholewheat flour sifted with 1$\frac{1}{2}$ teaspoons baking powder)
2 tablespoons milk
Topping
1 tablespoon lemon juice
1 tablespoon clear honey
4 tablespoons demerara sugar (U.S. 5 tablespoons brown sugar)

Cream the butter or margarine with the honey and sugar in a bowl until light and fluffy. Add the egg and lemon rind, beating well to blend. Fold in the lemon juice, flour and milk, blending well.

Spoon into a greased and lined 15 cm/6 inch round cake tin and level the surface. Bake in a preheated moderate oven (180°C, 350°F, Gas Mark 4) for about 40 minutes until firm and well risen. Turn out and allow to cool on a wire rack.

To make the topping, place the lemon juice and honey in a small pan and warm gently. Spoon over the cooling cake so that it soaks in. Sprinkle with the demerara sugar and leave until cold. Cut into wedges to serve.

Makes 1 × 15 cm/6 inch round cake

Soft honey cookies

(Illustrated below)

75 g/3 oz (U.S. 6 tablespoons) butter or margarine
100 g/4 oz (U.S. $\frac{1}{3}$ cup) set honey
225 g/8 oz (U.S. 2 cups) wholewheat flour
1 teaspoon baking powder
pinch of salt
50 g/2 oz demerara sugar (U.S. $\frac{1}{3}$ cup brown sugar)
1 teaspoon ground cinnamon
1 egg, beaten

Place the butter or margarine and honey in a pan and heat gently until melted.

Mix the flour with the baking powder, salt, sugar and cinnamon in a bowl. Add the warm honey mixture and egg. Mix well to blend.

Place heaped teaspoonfuls of the mixture on to lightly greased baking trays. Bake in a preheated moderate oven (180°C, 350°F, Gas Mark 4) for about 15 minutes. Allow to cool on a wire rack.

Soft honey cookies are delicious eaten while still warm but will keep in an airtight tin for up to 1 week.

Makes 20

Left: *Lemon honey cake*
Centre: *Cherry and almond cake*
Right: *Soft honey cookies*

Pear galette

(Illustrated above)

350 g/12 oz plain flour (U.S. 3 cups all-purpose flour)
225 g/8 oz (U.S. 1 cup) butter
100 g/4 oz castor sugar (U.S. $\frac{1}{2}$ cup superfine sugar)
50 g/2 oz (U.S. $\frac{1}{2}$ cup) hazelnuts, finely chopped
300 ml/$\frac{1}{2}$ pint double cream (U.S. $1\frac{1}{4}$ cups heavy cream)
1 × 822 g/1 lb 13 oz can pear halves, drained
sifted icing sugar (U.S. confectioner's sugar) to dust
hazelnuts to decorate

Sift the flour into a bowl. Rub in (U.S. cut in) the butter until the mixture resembles fine breadcrumbs. Stir in the sugar and hazelnuts, blending well. Knead the mixture well to form a ball.

Divide the dough in half and roll out each half on a lightly floured surface to a 20 cm/8 inch round. Place on greased baking trays or in two greased or lined 20 cm/8 inch sandwich tins (U.S. layer cake pans). Prick thoroughly with a fork.

Bake in a preheated moderately hot oven (190 °C, 375 °F, Gas Mark 5) for 20 minutes. Reduce the oven temperature to moderate (160 °C, 325 °F, Gas Mark 3) and bake for a further 20 minutes. Allow to cool in the tins for 5 minutes then carefully lift out on to a wire rack. Mark one round with a sharp knife into eight sections.

Whip the cream until it stands in soft peaks. Spread half of the cream over the unmarked round and top with the pears.

Cover with the second shortcake round and dust with the sugar. Pipe the remaining cream in swirls over the top of the galette. Decorate with hazelnuts. Serve lightly chilled. **Serves 8**

Orange curd bakewells

(Illustrated above)

Pastry
100 g/4 oz plain flour (U.S. 1 cup all-purpose flour)
pinch of salt
50 g/2 oz (U.S. ¼ cup) butter
1 tablespoon castor sugar (U.S. superfine sugar)
1 egg yolk
cold water
Filling
4 tablespoons (U.S. 5 tablespoons) orange curd
1 egg white
50 g/2 oz castor sugar (U.S. ¼ cup superfine sugar)
3 tablespoons (U.S. 4 tablespoons) ground almonds
few drops of almond essence (U.S. almond extract)
2 tablespoons flaked almonds (U.S. slivered almonds)

To make the pastry, mix the flour with the salt in a bowl. Rub in (U.S. cut in) the butter until the mixture resembles fine breadcrumbs. Stir in the sugar, blending well. Add the egg yolk and sufficient cold water to bind to a firm but pliable dough.

Roll out on a lightly floured surface and stamp out twelve rounds using a 9 cm/3½ inch cutter. Use to line twelve tartlet tins. Spoon the orange curd equally into the base of each tart.

Whisk the egg white until it stands in stiff peaks. Fold in the sugar, ground almonds and almond essence. Spoon into the pastry cases, completely covering the orange curd. Sprinkle with the flaked almonds.

Bake in a preheated moderate oven (180°C, 350°F, Gas Mark 4) for 20–25 minutes until golden. Allow to cool on a wire rack. **Makes 12**

Crunchy ginger bars

(Illustrated below)

100 g/4 oz (U.S. 1 cup) plain wholewheat flour
1 teaspoon baking powder
½ teaspoon bicarbonate of soda (U.S. baking soda)
1½ teaspoons ground ginger
100 g/4 oz Summer Orchard cereal
1 rounded tablespoon golden syrup (U.S. corn syrup)
100 g/4 oz (U.S. ½ cup) butter or margarine
100 g/4 oz demerara sugar (U.S. ½ cup brown sugar)

Mix the flour with the baking powder, bicarbonate of soda, ginger and cereal, blending well.

Place the syrup, butter or margarine and sugar in a pan and heat gently until melted. Stir into the dry ingredients and mix well to blend.

Spoon into a lightly greased 18 cm/7 inch square cake tin and level the surface. Bake in a preheated moderate oven (180°C, 350°F, Gas Mark 4) for 15–20 minutes. Leave to cool in the tin for 5 minutes.

Using a sharp knife, mark into twelve bars. Allow to cool, then remove from the tin. **Makes 12**

Wholewheat corn scones

(Illustrated below)

225 g/8 oz (U.S. 2 cups) wholewheat flour
4 teaspoons baking powder
¼ teaspoon salt
50 g/2 oz (U.S. ¼ cup) butter or margarine
1 tablespoon bran
1 × 198 g/7 oz can sweetcorn kernels (U.S. whole kernel corn)
100 ml/4 fl oz (U.S. ½ cup) milk
milk to glaze

Sift the flour, baking powder and salt into a bowl. Add any bran left in the sieve. Rub in (U.S. cut in) the butter or margarine until the mixture resembles fine bread-crumbs.

Stir in the bran, sweetcorn kernels and their juice and milk, and mix to a soft but manageable dough.

Turn the dough on to a lightly floured surface and knead until smooth. Roll out to about 1 cm/½ inch thick-ness and stamp out twelve rounds with a 6 cm/2½ inch scone or biscuit cutter (U.S. cookie cutter), re-rolling as necessary.

Place on a greased baking tray and glaze with milk. Bake in a preheated hot oven (220°C, 425°F, Gas Mark 7) for 18 minutes or until well risen and golden brown. Allow to cool on a wire rack. **Makes 12**

Wholesome barm brack

(Illustrated right)

450 ml/¾ pint (U.S. 2 cups) cold tea
200 g/7 oz (U.S. 1 cup) soft brown sugar
350 g/12 oz (U.S. 2 cups) mixed dried fruit
275 g/10 oz (U.S. 2½ cups) self-raising wheatmeal flour
1 egg, beaten
2 tablespoons honey, warmed to glaze

Place the tea, sugar and dried fruit in a bowl. Cover and leave to soak overnight.

Stir the tea mixture into the flour with the egg until smooth. Spoon into a greased 450 g/1 lb loaf tin. Bake in a preheated moderate oven (180 °C, 350 °F, Gas Mark 4) for 1½–1¾ hours.

While still hot, brush the loaf with honey. Transfer to a wire rack to cool. Serve cold, sliced and buttered if liked. **Makes about 12 slices**

Below left: *Crunchy ginger bars*
Below: *Wholewheat corn scones*
Right: *Wholesome barm brack*

Carob cream cake

(Illustrated above)

75 g/3 oz (U.S. 6 tablespoons) butter
7 digestive biscuits (U.S. graham crackers), crushed
100 g/4 oz (U.S. ½ cup) brown sugar
1 egg, beaten
150 g/5 oz (U.S. 1¼ cups) self-raising wheatmeal flour
15 g/½ oz (U.S. 2 tablespoons) carob powder
150 ml/¼ pint (U.S. ⅔ cup) milk
whipped cream to decorate

Melt 25 g/1 oz (U.S. 2 tablespoons) of the butter in a pan. Add the biscuit crumbs, blending well. Press on to the base of an 18 cm/7 inch loose-bottomed cake tin.

Cream the remaining butter with the sugar in a bowl until light and fluffy. Gradually add the egg and fold in the flour and carob powder. Stir in the milk and spoon on to the biscuit base.

Bake in a preheated moderate oven (180°C, 350°F, Gas Mark 4) until well risen and cooked, about 30–35 minutes. Allow to cool in the tin.

To serve, turn out and place on a serving plate. Decorate with swirls of whipped cream. **Serves 8**

Carrot and pecan loaf

(Illustrated above)

75 g/3 oz (U.S. ½ cup) soft brown sugar
75 g/3 oz (U.S. 6 tablespoons) butter
175 g/6 oz (U.S. 1½ cups) carrots, peeled and grated
1 teaspoon ground mixed spice
1½ tablespoons water
1 egg, beaten
75 g/3 oz (U.S. ¾ cup) pecan nuts, chopped
175 g/6 oz (U.S. 1½ cups) self-raising wholewheat flour
½ teaspoon salt
1 tablespoon milk
pecan halves to decorate

Place the sugar, butter, carrots, spice and water in a pan. Heat gently to dissolve the sugar, bring to the boil and cook for 3 minutes, stirring constantly. Remove from the heat and allow to cool. Add the beaten egg and pecans, blending well. Fold in the flour, salt and milk, mixing well.

Spoon into a greased and base-lined 450 g/1 lb loaf tin and level the surface. Decorate with a few pecan halves placed over the top edge of the loaf. Bake in a preheated moderate oven (180°C, 350°F, Gas Mark 4) for 1 hour.

Allow to cool in the tin for 10 minutes then turn out to cool on a wire rack. Serve sliced and buttered.
Makes 1 × 450 g/1 lb loaf

Sesame flapjacks

(Illustrated above)

100 g/4 oz (U.S. ½ cup) butter or margarine
25 g/1 oz (U.S. 2 tablespoons) brown sugar
4 tablespoons golden syrup (U.S. 5 tablespoons
corn syrup)
pinch of salt
200 g/7 oz (U.S. 2 cups) rolled oats
25 g/1 oz (U.S. ¼ cup) sesame seeds

Place the butter or margarine, sugar and syrup in a pan. Heat gently to melt. Add the salt, oats and sesame seeds, blending well.

Spread into a greased 28 × 18 cm/11 × 7 inch shallow cake tin. Bake in a preheated moderately hot oven (190°C, 375°F, Gas Mark 5) until golden and firm to the touch, about 30 minutes.

Allow to cool slightly, then cut into fingers. Allow to cool completely in the tin. **Makes about 20**

Bran, hazelnut and oat slice

(Illustrated above)

100 g/4 oz (U.S. ½ cup) butter
100 g/4 oz (U.S. ⅔ cup) muscovado sugar
2 eggs
2 tablespoons milk
75 g/3 oz (U.S. ¾ cup) plain wholewheat flour
2 teaspoons baking powder
50 g/2 oz (U.S. ⅔ cup) rolled oats
3 tablespoons (U.S. 4 tablespoons) bran
50 g/2 oz (U.S. ½ cup) hazelnuts, chopped
Topping
100 g/4 oz (U.S. ½ cup) cream cheese
2 teaspoons sifted icing sugar (U.S. confectioner's sugar)
3 tablespoons (U.S. 4 tablespoons) orange juice

Cream the butter with the sugar in a bowl until light and fluffy. Blend in the eggs and milk. Fold in the flour, baking powder, oats, bran and hazelnuts, blending well.

Spoon and spread evenly into a greased and lined 20 cm/8 inch square shallow cake tin. Bake in a preheated moderately hot oven (190°C, 375°F, Gas Mark 5) for 20–25 minutes until firm and springy to the touch. Allow to cool slightly, then turn out and allow to cool on a wire rack.

To make the topping, beat the cream cheese with the icing sugar and orange juice. Swirl over the cake and cut into slices to serve. **Makes about 16 slices**

Entertaining

A light luncheon dish to feed a special friend; a gastronomic feast to impress a selected few; or a special ritualistic high day or holiday festive meal are just some entertaining occasions when effort, impressions and appearances really count.

This section therefore devotes itself un-ashamedly to cater for such times when luxury is often the keynote to success – few nurture feelings of guilt at serving high-price foods flown in from afar on such auspicious occasions. Hand-in-glove also goes the use of perhaps more unusual foods like celeriac in a blue cheese bake or mustard to be savoured alone in a creamy soup. The realization that a lengthy prep-aration dish is justified invites one to make neat Red Cabbage Parcels or Dolmas or a special time-intensive Chestnut Yule Log and the high cost of ingredients in making Aubergine Pâté out of season all the more enticing.

Such moments also give the cook a certain degree of timing accuracy that can never be repeated on other occasions, so sensitive dishes like soufflés can come to the fore and can be made in the safe knowledge that food time can be called when the dish is at its best.

Choose dishes and whole menus carefully to suit the occasion and the guests you expect – always erring on the side of safety by under-estimating rather than over-estimating your skills. It is always better to cook a few dishes well than too many with mediocre results. Prepare as many ahead as possible leaving only last minute salad, vegetable and sauce additions for the day – that way you should also have time to enjoy your guests and the food.

Above left: *Lasagne with courgettes and corn (recipe page 176)*
Above right: *Aubergine pâté (recipe page 176)*
Below right: *Fresh fruit shells (recipe page 183)*

Aubergine pâté

(Illustrated on pages 174–175)

2 medium aubergines (U.S. eggplants)
1 × 62.5 g/2½ oz packet butter with herbs and garlic
1 tablespoon lemon juice
½ teaspoon ground cumin
6 black olives, stoned and chopped (U.S. 6 ripe olives, pitted and chopped) (optional)
To garnish
lemon slices
parsley sprigs
warm pitta bread to serve

Prick the aubergine skins with a fork and place on a baking tray. Bake in a preheated moderately hot oven (190°C, 375°F, Gas Mark 5) until soft and wrinkled, about 45 minutes.

Cut in half and scoop out the soft flesh. Place in a blender with the butter with herbs and garlic, lemon juice and cumin. Purée until smooth.

Spoon into a serving dish and sprinkle with the olives. Garnish with lemon slices and parsley sprigs. Serve warm or chilled with warm pitta bread. **Serves 4**

Tandoori dahl kebabs

2 tablespoons oil
1 onion, peeled and very finely chopped
3 garlic cloves, peeled and crushed
2 stalks celery, scrubbed and very finely chopped
1 large carrot, peeled and grated
225 g/8 oz (U.S. 1 cup) lentils
2 tablespoons tomato purée
4 teaspoons tandoori spice mixture
600 ml/1 pint (U.S. 2½ cups) vegetable stock or water
25 g/1 oz (U.S. ½ cup) wholewheat breadcrumbs
50 g/2 oz (U.S. ½ cup) walnuts, finely chopped
2 tablespoons chopped fresh parsley
1 egg, beaten
salt and freshly ground black pepper
225 g/8 oz (U.S. 1 cup) thick set natural yogurt
½ cucumber, peeled and grated

Heat the oil in a large pan. Add the onion, two thirds of the garlic, the celery and carrot and cook until softened, about 5 minutes. Stir in the lentils, tomato purée. three quarters of the tandoori spice and the stock or water, blending well. Bring to the boil, cover and simmer for about 1 hour, stirring occasionally, until the mixture is very thick and no excess liquid remains.

Add the breadcrumbs, walnuts, parsley, egg and salt and pepper to taste. Allow to cool slightly then divide into 8 portions and shape each around a wooden skewer to make long thick sausage-shaped rissoles. Sprinkle with the remaining tandoori spice. Cook under a preheated hot grill for 4–5 minutes, turning frequently.

To make the sauce, mix the yogurt with the remaining garlic and the cucumber. Serve with the kebabs. **Serves 4**

Lasagne with courgettes and corn

(Illustrated on pages 174–175)

175 g/6 oz wholewheat lasagne
2 tablespoons oil
1 onion, peeled and sliced
225 g/8 oz courgettes (U.S. zucchini), trimmed and sliced
225 g/8 oz tomatoes, skinned and coarsely chopped
1 × 335 g/11.8 oz can sweetcorn kernels (U.S. whole kernel corn), drained
2 tablespoons chopped fresh mint
salt and freshly ground black pepper
5 tablespoons (U.S. 6 tablespoons) white wine or vegetable stock
300 ml/½ pint (U.S. 1¼ cups) Cheese Sauce (see page 84)
To garnish
raw onion rings
mint sprigs

Cook the lasagne in a pan of boiling salted water according to the packet instructions. Drain thoroughly.

Meanwhile, heat the oil in a pan. Add the onion and cook until softened, about 5 minutes.

Add the courgettes, tomatoes, sweetcorn, mint and salt and pepper to taste, blending well. Simmer gently for 20 minutes. Add the wine or stock and simmer for a further 10 minutes.

Layer the sweetcorn mixture and lasagne in a shallow ovenproof dish, finishing with a layer of pasta. Cover with the cheese sauce. Bake in a preheated moderately hot oven (190°C, 375°F, Gas Mark 5) until golden, about 35 minutes. Garnish and serve hot with a crisp salad. **Serves 4**

Cream of mustard soup with Cheese soda bread

Cream of mustard soup

(Illustrated below)

25 g/1 oz (U.S. 2 tablespoons) butter
1 bunch spring onions (U.S. scallions), chopped
1 tablespoon mustard powder
1 tablespoon flour
600 ml/1 pint (U.S. 2½ cups) vegetable stock
2 tablespoons French mustard
½ teaspoon lemon juice
2 egg yolks
300 ml/½ pint single cream (U.S. 1¼ cups light cream)
salt and freshly ground black pepper
chopped spring onion (U.S. scallion) to garnish

Melt the butter in a pan. Add the spring onions, reserving a few to garnish, and cook for 5 minutes.

Stir in the mustard powder and flour, blending well. Cook for 1 minute, stirring constantly. Stir in the stock, mustard and lemon juice. Simmer gently for 5 minutes.

Beat the egg yolks with the cream and salt and pepper to taste. Stir into the soup and cook over a gentle heat, stirring constantly until thickened. *Do not allow to boil.* Sprinkle with remaining spring onion. **Serves 4**

Cheese soda bread

(Illustrated below)

225 g/8 oz plain white or wholewheat flour (U.S. 2 cups all-purpose or wholewheat flour)
1 teaspoon mustard powder
½ teaspoon salt
¼ teaspoon bicarbonate of soda (U.S. baking soda)
¼ teaspoon cream of tartar
½ teaspoon dried sage
100 g/4 oz (U.S. 1 cup) Cheddar cheese, grated
175 ml/6 fl oz (U.S. ¾ cup) buttermilk or fresh milk with 1 teaspoon lemon juice added

Mix the flour with the mustard, salt, bicarbonate of soda, cream of tartar and sage in a bowl. Stir in 75 g/3 oz (U.S. ¾ cup) of the cheese, blending well.

Add the buttermilk and mix to a firm dough. Knead on a lightly floured surface and shape to make a neat round. Using a sharp knife, mark into eight sections.

Place on a baking tray and sprinkle with the remaining cheese. Bake in a preheated moderately hot oven (200°C, 400°F, Gas Mark 6) for 30 minutes or until golden and firm to the touch. Serve warm. **Serves 4**

Red cabbage parcels

(Illustrated opposite)

100 g/4 oz (U.S. ⅔ cup) bulghur wheat
5 tablespoons (U.S. 6 tablespoons) boiling water
8 red cabbage leaves
1 dessert apple, peeled, cored and chopped
1 onion, peeled and finely chopped
25 g/1 oz sultanas (U.S. 2 tablespoons golden raisins)
100 g/4 oz (U.S. 1 cup) Cheddar cheese, grated
5 tablespoons (U.S. 6 tablespoons) apple syrup
apple slices to garnish

Place the wheat and boiling water in a bowl. Fork through gently and leave to stand for 15 minutes to allow the wheat to swell.

Blanch the red cabbage leaves in a pan of boiling water for 1 minute. Plunge into cold water, then drain thoroughly and dry on absorbent kitchen towel.

Add the apple, onion, sultanas and cheese to the wheat, blending well.

Spoon equal amounts of the wheat mixture into the centre of each cabbage leaf. Fold over the leaves to enclose the filling and form a parcel. Place, seam sides down, in a greased shallow ovenproof dish.

Make up the apple syrup to 200 ml/7 fl oz with boiling water and pour over the red cabbage parcels. Cover with foil. Bake in a preheated moderately hot oven (190°C, 375°F, Gas Mark 5) for 1 hour, basting with the juices halfway through cooking.

Garnish and serve hot as a main course for two or as a vegetable accompaniment for four. **Serves 2–4**

Blue cheese, celeriac and onion bake

(Illustrated opposite)

450 g/1 lb celeriac, peeled and thinly sliced
100 g/4 oz mature Cheddar cheese (U.S. 1 cup sharp Cheddar cheese), grated
1 large onion, peeled and finely chopped
150 ml/¼ pint (U.S. ⅔ cup) milk
1 × 62.5 g/2½ oz packet butter with blue cheese
50 g/2 oz (U.S. 1 cup) fresh wholewheat breadcrumbs
25 g/1 oz (U.S. ¼ cup) sesame seeds
parsley sprig to garnish

Layer the celeriac, cheese and onion in a greased shallow ovenproof dish. Pour over the milk.

Melt the butter with blue cheese in a pan. Stir in the breadcrumbs and sesame seeds. Sprinkle on top of the celeriac mixture. Cover with foil.

Bake in a preheated moderately hot oven (190°C, 375°F, Gas Mark 5) for 1¼ hours or until the celeriac is tender, removing the foil for the final 15 minutes cooking time. Garnish and serve hot as a tasty vegetable accompaniment. **Serves 4**

Pecan croquettes

100 g/4 oz (U.S. 1 cup) pecans, very finely chopped
75 g/3 oz (U.S. 1½ cups) wholewheat breadcrumbs
1 small leek, trimmed and very finely chopped
50 g/2 oz (U.S. ½ cup) Cheddar cheese, grated
1 tablespoon snipped chives
salt and freshly ground black pepper
1 large egg, beaten
1–2 tablespoons milk
2 tablespoons oil
1 recipe Thick Waldorf Relish (see page 88)

Mix the pecans with the breadcrumbs, leek, cheese, chives and salt and pepper to taste. Add the egg and milk and bind together to make a firm mixture.

Divide into 10–12 pieces and roll each into a small croquette.

Heat the oil in a pan. Add the croquettes and cook gently for about 10 minutes, turning regularly so that the croquettes brown evenly. Drain on absorbent kitchen paper.

Serve the croquettes warm with the relish as a tasty starter, to serve with drinks if liked, or part of a main course buffet spread. **Serves 4**

Above and below: Red cabbage parcels
Centre: Blue cheese, celeriac and onion bake

Crunchy topped vegetable soufflé

(Illustrated opposite)

100 g/4 oz (U.S. ½ cup) butter
225 g/8 oz leeks, trimmed, washed and thinly sliced
25 g/1 oz (U.S. ¼ cup) wholewheat flour
150 ml/¼ pint (U.S. ⅔ cup) soured cream
4 tablespoons (U.S. 5 tablespoons) natural yogurt
100 g/4 oz mature Cheddar cheese (U.S. 1 cup sharp
Cheddar cheese), grated
1 × 298 g/10.5 oz can cream style corn
275 g/10 oz cold boiled potatoes, coarsely grated
5 eggs, separated
grated nutmeg
salt and freshly ground black pepper

Melt the butter in a pan. Add the leeks and cook until softened, about 8–10 minutes.

Stir in the flour, blending well. Remove from the heat and blend in the soured cream and yogurt. Return to the heat and cook gently, stirring constantly, for 5 minutes until thickened.

Add 75 g/3 oz (U.S. ¾ cup) of the cheese and beat well to blend. Add the cream style corn, potatoes, egg yolks, nutmeg and salt and pepper to taste, mixing well.

Whisk the egg whites until they stand in stiff peaks and fold into the potato mixture with a metal spoon. Spoon into a greased 2.25 litre/4 pint (U.S. 5 pint) soufflé dish and sprinkle with the remaining cheese.

Bake in a preheated moderately hot oven (190°C, 375°F, Gas Mark 5) for about 50 minutes. Serve at once.

Crunchy Topped Vegetable Soufflé is delicious served with chopped tomatoes sprinkled with a little chopped fresh basil. **Serves 4**

Variation

Leeks have been chosen as the basic flavouring vegetable in the above soufflé recipe but thinly sliced onion, carrot, celery, peppers, fennel, kohlrabi and artichoke hearts could also be used singly or in combination. For additional flavour, dried herbs may be added with the cheese, about 1–2 teaspoons would give a good flavour or a herb-flavoured hard cheese could be used. Half of the potatoes may also be replaced with cold boiled and coarsely grated parsnips (U.S. rutabagas) if liked.

Dolmas

(Illustrated opposite)

8 large outer cabbage leaves
1 tablespoon oil
1 onion, peeled and chopped
1 garlic clove, peeled and crushed
2 stalks celery, scrubbed and chopped
15 g/½ oz (U.S. 1 tablespoon) sunflower seeds
50 g/2 oz (U.S. ½ cup) pine nuts
50 g/2 oz sultanas (U.S. ⅓ cup golden raisins)
175 g/6 oz (U.S. scant 1 cup) brown rice, cooked
1 × 335 g/11.8 oz can sweetcorn kernels (U.S. whole
kernel corn), drained
Speedy Tomato Sauce
1 × 398 g/14 oz can peeled tomatoes, coarsely chopped
1 bay leaf
2 stalks celery, scrubbed and chopped
1 tablespoon chopped fresh parsley

Blanch the cabbage leaves in a pan of boiling water for 2 minutes. Drain thoroughly.

Heat the oil in a pan. Add the onion and garlic and cook until softened, about 5 minutes. Add the celery, blending well and cook for a further 5 minutes. Stir in the sunflower seeds, pine nuts, sultanas, rice and sweetcorn.

Spread the cabbage leaves open and divide the corn mixture between the leaves. Roll up, tucking in the ends to make neat 'parcels'. Place closely together in a shallow ovenproof dish.

Meanwhile to make the sauce, place the tomatoes, bay leaf, celery and parsley in a pan. Simmer gently for 10 minutes. Remove and discard the bay leaf. Purée the sauce in a blender or food processor until smooth or pour through a fine sieve.

Pour the sauce over the dolmas. Bake in a preheated moderately hot oven (200°C, 400°F, Gas Mark 6) for 30 minutes. Serve hot. **Serves 4**

Above: *Crunchy topped vegetable soufflé*
Below: *Dolmas*

Stuffed peppers

(Illustrated opposite)

4 red, green or yellow peppers
1 tablespoon oil
1 onion, peeled and chopped
1 small cucumber, peeled and chopped
1 × 198 g/7 oz can sweetcorn kernels (u.s. whole kernel corn), drained
100 g/4 oz vegetable suet
225 g/8 oz tomatoes, skinned, seeded and chopped
celery salt and freshly ground black pepper
100 g/4 oz (u.s. 1 cup) Cheddar cheese, grated
parsley sprigs to garnish

Cut a slice from the stalk end of each pepper and core. Blanch the peppers in a pan of boiling water for 1 minute, then plunge into cold water. Drain thoroughly.

Heat the oil in a pan. Add the onion and cucumber and fry for 5 minutes. Remove from the heat and add the sweetcorn, suet, tomatoes and celery salt and pepper to taste, blending well.

Spoon the mixture into the peppers evenly and stand them in an ovenproof dish. Sprinkle with the cheese.

Bake in a preheated moderate oven (180°C, 350°F, Gas Mark 4) for 15 minutes. Serve hot, garnished with parsley sprigs. **Serves 4**

Spinach and almond pancakes

1 recipe Pancake Batter (see page 156)
Filling
25 g/1 oz (u.s. 2 tablespoons) butter
25 g/1 oz plain flour ((u.s. $\frac{1}{4}$ cup all-purpose flour)
300 ml/$\frac{1}{2}$ pint (u.s. 1$\frac{1}{4}$ cups) milk
225 g/8 oz (u.s. 2 cups) Cheddar cheese, grated
225 g/8 oz (u.s. 1 cup) frozen spinach, cooked and well drained
pinch of grated nutmeg
50 g/2 oz (u.s. $\frac{1}{2}$ cup) blanched almonds, chopped
salt and freshly ground black pepper

Prepare the pancake batter and cook as on page 156 to make 8 pancakes. Keep warm.

To make the filling, place the butter, flour and milk in a pan. Heat gently, stirring constantly, until the butter melts. Bring to the boil, stirring constantly and cook for 2–3 minutes. Add the cheese, spinach, nutmeg, almonds and salt and pepper to taste, blending well until the cheese melts.

Divide the mixture evenly between the pancakes, roll up and place, seam-side down, in a shallow heatproof dish. Cook under a preheated hot grill until bubbly, about 5 minutes. Serve hot. **Serves 4**

Pissaladière

(Illustrated opposite)

Pastry
225 g/8 oz self-raising flour (u.s. 2 cups self-rising flour sifted with 1$\frac{1}{2}$ teaspoons baking powder)
75 g/3 oz (u.s. 6 tablespoons) vegetable suet
cold water
Filling
2 tablespoons oil
1 large onion, peeled and finely chopped
1 garlic clove, peeled and crushed
450 g/1 lb tomatoes, skinned, seeded and chopped
1 teaspoon chopped fresh basil
salt and freshly ground black pepper
100 g/4 oz courgettes (u.s. zucchini), trimmed, sliced and blanched
50 g/2 oz (u.s. $\frac{1}{2}$ cup) Gruyère cheese, grated
50 g/2 oz anchovy fillets
7 black olives, stoned and halved (u.s. 7 ripe olives, pitted and halved)

To make the pastry base, mix the flour with the suet and sufficient cold water to make a firm but pliable dough. Roll out on a lightly floured surface to a 25 cm/10 inch round. Place on a greased baking tray.

To make the filling, heat the oil in a pan. Add the onion and garlic and fry until softened, about 5 minutes. Add the tomatoes, basil and salt and pepper to taste, blending well. Simmer gently for 10 minutes. Allow to cool.

Spread evenly on top of the pastry base and arrange courgette slices around the edge. Sprinkle with cheese and arrange a lattice of anchovies and olives on top.

Bake in a preheated moderately hot oven (190°C, 375°F, Gas Mark 5) for 30 minutes. **Serves 6–8**

Above left: Stuffed peppers
Above right: Pissaladière
Below: Fresh fruit shells

Fresh fruit shells

(Illustrated above, on pages 174–175 and as frontispiece)

Pastry
225 g/8 oz (U.S. 2 cups) self-raising wheatmeal flour
pinch of salt
100 g/4 oz (U.S. $\frac{3}{4}$ cup) vegetable suet
1 small egg, beaten
cold water to mix
beaten egg to glaze
sugar to sprinkle
Filling
4 egg yolks
150 g/5 oz (U.S. $\frac{1}{2}$ cup plus 2 tablespoons) sugar
75 g/3 oz (U.S. $\frac{3}{4}$ cup) flour
1 litre/1$\frac{3}{4}$ pints (U.S. 4$\frac{1}{4}$ cups) milk
few drops of vanilla essence (U.S. vanilla extract)
Topping
prepared fresh fruit in season
warmed honey to glaze

To make the pastry, mix the flour with the salt and suet. Bind together with the egg and sufficient cold water to make a firm but pliable dough.

Roll out on a lightly floured surface and use to line 6–8 large individual tartlet tins or scallop shells. Glaze with beaten egg and sprinkle with sugar. Prick well with a fork.

Bake in a preheated moderately hot oven (190 °C, 375 °F, Gas Mark 5) for 10–15 minutes until crisp and golden. Allow to cool on a wire rack.

To make the filling, whisk the egg yolks, sugar and flour in a bowl. Heat the milk and vanilla essence in a pan to just below boiling point to scald. Pour slowly over the egg mixture, blending well. Return the mixture to the saucepan and cook for 3–5 minutes until smooth and thickened. Allow to cool.

Pipe the filling into the pastry shells. Decorate the pastry cream-filled shells with prepared fresh fruit in season, then glaze with warmed honey. Serve on the day of making. **Makes 6–8**

Strawberry shortcake

(Illustrated below)

350 g/12 oz plain flour (u.s. 3 cups all-purpose flour)
225 g/8 oz (u.s. 1 cup) butter
100 g/4 oz castor sugar (u.s. $\frac{1}{2}$ cup superfine sugar)
300 ml/$\frac{1}{2}$ pint double cream (u.s. 1$\frac{1}{4}$ cups heavy cream)
450 g/1 lb strawberries, hulled and halved
few strawberries to decorate

Sift the flour into a bowl. Rub in (u.s. cut in) the butter until the mixture resembles fine breadcrumbs. Stir in the sugar and knead together lightly to form a pliable dough.

Divide in half and roll out each piece on a lightly floured surface to a 20 cm/8 inch round. Place on greased baking trays, crimp the edges decoratively and prick with a fork.

Bake in a preheated moderately hot oven (190°C, 375°F, Gas Mark 5) for 20 minutes. Reduce the oven temperature to moderate (160°C, 325°F, Gas Mark 3) and bake for a further 20 minutes. Allow to cool on the trays.

Whip the cream until it stands in soft peaks. Pipe half over one of the shortcake rounds and top with the strawberries. Top with the second shortcake round.

Place the remaining cream in a piping bag (u.s. pastry bag) fitted with a large star-shaped nozzle and pipe swirls around the top edge of the shortcake. Decorate with a few strawberries and serve on day of making, lightly chilled. **Serves 6–8**

Variations
Strawberry and kiwi shortcake Prepare and cook as before but use 350 g/12 oz (u.s. 2$\frac{1}{3}$ cups) strawberries with 2 ripe kiwi fruit (u.s. Chinese gooseberries) instead of all strawberries. Peel the kiwi fruit and slice thinly for use.
Raspberry and orange shortcake Prepare and cook as before but use 450 g/1 lb raspberries tossed in a little grated orange rind instead of the strawberries.

Pineapple fruit salad

(Illustrated below)

1 large fresh pineapple
2 large oranges, peeled, pith removed and cut into
segments or slices
4 plums, halved, stoned (U.S. pitted) and sliced
2 green dessert apples, cored and sliced
1 tablespoon brown sugar
2 teaspoons lemon juice
3 tablespoons (U.S. 4 tablespoons) apple juice or cider
ice-cream to serve

Halve the pineapple lengthways. Using a sharp knife, carefully remove the flesh, leaving the shells intact. Remove the pineapple core and discard. Chop the flesh into bite-sized pieces.

Mix the pineapple pieces with the orange segments, plums and apple, blending well.

Mix the sugar with the lemon juice and apple juice or cider until dissolved – heat gently in a small pan if necessary. Pour over the fruit and toss to coat.

Spoon back into the pineapple shells. Serve lightly chilled, topped with a few scoops of ice-cream. **Serves 4**

Butterscotch pudding

juice of 1 orange
50 g/2 oz (U.S. $\frac{1}{4}$ cup) butter
1 tablespoon light muscovado sugar
2 oranges, peeled, pith removed and sliced
100 g/4 oz (U.S. $\frac{1}{2}$ cup) margarine
100 g/4 oz (U.S. $\frac{2}{3}$ cup) muscovado sugar
2 eggs
175 g/6 oz self-raising flour (U.S. $1\frac{1}{2}$ cups self-rising
flour sifted with $1\frac{1}{2}$ teaspoons baking powder)
1 teaspoon baking powder
5 tablespoons (U.S. 6 tablespoons) milk

Place the orange juice, butter and light muscovado sugar in a pan. Stir over a gentle heat until melted. Pour into a 20 cm/8 inch round non-stick tin. Arrange the orange slices decoratively on top.

Beat the margarine with the muscovado sugar until light and fluffy. Beat in the eggs then gradually add the flour, baking powder and milk to produce a mixture with a soft dropping consistency.

Spoon over and spread the orange slices. Bake in a moderate oven (180°C, 350°F, Gas Mark 4) for 1 hour. To serve, turn out and drizzle with a little yogurt. **Serves 6**

Raspberry yogurt ice-cream

(Illustrated opposite)

300 ml/½ pint (U.S. 1¼ cups) thick set natural yogurt
225 g/8 oz raspberries, hulled
150 ml/¼ pint (U.S. ⅔ cup) clear honey
1 teaspoon lemon juice
150 ml/¼ pint double cream (U.S. ⅔ cup heavy cream)
To decorate
raspberries
mint sprigs

Place the yogurt, raspberries, honey and lemon juice in a blender or food processor and purée until smooth.

Whip the cream until it stands in soft peaks. Fold into the raspberry mixture with a metal spoon.

Spoon into a rigid freezer container and freeze until firm. Serve scooped into dessert glasses. Decorate with a few fresh raspberries and mint sprigs. **Serves 6**

Variations

Banana yogurt ice-cream Prepare as before but use 2 large ripe peeled bananas instead of the raspberries. Serve decorated with fresh fruit in season.

Strawberry yogurt ice-cream Prepare as before but use hulled strawberries instead of the raspberries. Serve decorated with a few fresh strawberries and chopped nuts.

Raspberry and pistachio yogurt ice-cream Prepare as before but add 25 g/1 oz (U.S. ¼ cup) finely chopped pistachio nuts with the cream.

Gooseberry yogurt ice-cream Prepare as before but use 175 ml/6 fl oz (U.S. ¾ cup) unsweetened gooseberry purée instead of the raspberries. Add a little additional honey or sugar if the gooseberries are very tart. Serve decorated with sprigs of fresh mint.

Maraschino cherry yogurt ice-cream Prepare as before but use 50–75 g/2–3 oz (U.S. ½ cup) maraschino cherries and 1 tablespoon of their juice instead of the raspberries.

Festive mince pies

(Illustrated on page 188)

350 g/12 oz (U.S. 3 cups) wholewheat flour
pinch of salt
75 g/3 oz (U.S. 6 tablespoons) butter or margarine
75 g/3 oz (U.S. 6 tablespoons) vegetable fat
about 5 tablespoons (U.S. 6 tablespoons) iced water
450 g/1 lb mincemeat
icing sugar (U.S. confectioner's sugar) to dust

To make the pastry, mix the flour with the salt in a bowl. Rub the butter or margarine and vegetable fat into the flour until the mixture resembles fine breadcrumbs. Add the water and bind to a firm but pliable dough.

Roll out the pastry on a lightly floured surface and stamp out about 20 rounds using a 7.5 cm/3 inch cutter. Use to line greased tartlet tins.

Re-roll the remaining pastry and use to stamp out about 20 lids, with a star-shaped cutter. Spoon the mincemeat evenly into the tartlets and top with the lids.

Bake in a preheated moderately hot oven (190°C, 375°F, Gas Mark 5) for 25 minutes. Allow to cool on a wire rack.

Serve warm or cold dusted with icing sugar.

Makes about 20

Above: Raspberry yogurt ice-cream
Below: Banana yogurt ice-cream

Chestnut yule log

(Illustrated above)

3 eggs
100 g/4 oz castor sugar (U.S. $\frac{1}{2}$ cup superfine sugar)
few drops rum or vanilla essence (U.S. extract)
75 g/3 oz self-raising flour (U.S. $\frac{3}{4}$ cup self-rising flour
sifted with $\frac{3}{4}$ teaspoon baking powder)
7 g/$\frac{1}{4}$ oz (U.S. 1 tablespoon) carob powder or 15 g/$\frac{1}{2}$ oz
(U.S. 2 tablespoons) cocoa powder dissolved in
1 tablespoon hot water
25 g/1 oz (U.S. 2 tablespoons) butter, melted
castor sugar (U.S. superfine sugar) to dust
225 g/8 oz (U.S. 1 cup) sweetened chestnut purée
50 g/2 oz plain chocolate (U.S. 2 squares semi-sweet
chocolate), melted
150 ml/$\frac{1}{4}$ pint double cream (U.S. $\frac{2}{3}$ cup heavy
cream)
holly sprigs to decorate

Whisk the eggs with the sugar and rum or vanilla essence in a bowl until very pale and thick. Fold in the flour and dissolved carob powder or cocoa powder, blending well. Stir in the melted butter.

Spoon the mixture evenly into a greased and lined 28 × 18 cm/11 × 7 inch Swiss roll tin (U.S. jelly roll pan).

Bake in a preheated hot oven (220 °C, 425 °F, Gas Mark 7) for 10 minutes.

Turn out on to a piece of greaseproof paper (U.S. waxed paper) lightly dusted with castor sugar. Quickly trim away the hard edges with a knife, then roll up, using the paper as a guide to turn the roll with the paper enclosed. Allow to cool.

Meanwhile, whisk the chestnut purée into the melted chocolate. Whip the cream until it stands in soft peaks, then whisk into the chestnut mixture.

Unroll the log, remove the paper and spread with about one third of the chestnut filling. Roll up gently. Coat the top and side of the log with the remaining chestnut mixture and fork lightly.

Serve lightly chilled, decorated with holly sprigs.
Serves 8

Centre: Chestnut yule log
Right: *Festive mince pies (recipe page 186)*

Index

189